AMERICAN PROPHET

The Story of Joseph Smith

HEIDI S. SWINTON

Based on the documentary by Lee Groberg

Shadow Mountain

Salt Lake City, Utah

To Jeffrey
and all our Smith ancestors

Library of Congress Cataloging-in-Publication Data

Swinton, Heidi S., 1948–
    American prophet : the story of Joseph Smith / Heidi S. Swinton.
        p.   cm.
    Includes bibliographical references and index.
    ISBN 1-57345-543-1
    1. Smith, Joseph, 1805–1844. 2. Mormons—United States Biography.
    I. Title.
    BX8695.S6S86   1999
    289.3'092—dc21
    [B]   99-23253
                                                  CIP

42316-6436

Printed in the United States of America
10   9   8   7   6   5   4   3   2   1

CONTENTS

PREFACE

JOSEPH SMITH'S story is a saga of heartache and bloodshed, faith and courage, resilience, devotion, and drive that is without match in the American religious experience. Yet for more than 150 years historians and writers have wrestled with its place and its message.

Joseph Smith was controversial in his day, and still the questions continue to stir the cauldrons of spiritual thought. Did he talk with God? Did he receive revelations of Divine will? Was he a seer, a visionary? Did he heal the sick? Translate scriptures from gold plates? And what about the angels? To declare him a prophet is to put him in the context of Isaiah, Elijah, John the Baptist, and Joshua.

To his faithful followers he was the "man who communed with Jehovah,"[1] and they came, "one of a city and two of a family," to join him in Zion (Jeremiah 3:14).

Life was never easy for this New England transplant. Opposition dogged Joseph all his days. His detractors labeled him a vile impostor, a charlatan. Friends and followers turned against him, accusing him of being a false prophet or a fallen one. He was physically attacked, poisoned, arrested, and jailed—not once, but often. Finally, at Carthage Jail in June 1844, Joseph was gunned down by a mob.

There were those who thought that killing the prophet would destroy the Church he led and snuff out his legacy as well. Not so. Today, The Church of Jesus Christ of Latter-day Saints, founded by Joseph Smith in 1830 with a fledgling band of believers about fifty strong, is considered the fastest growing religion in America.

This book joins with the television documentary *American Prophet: The Story of Joseph Smith*, produced by Lee B. Groberg and narrated by Gregory Peck, to tell the story of this singular figure in our nation's religious history. I thank Lee for giving me the opportunity to write both the book and the documentary script. I have tried to portray Joseph through the eyes of those who knew him personally and those who have studied his life and his times.

Journal and newspaper accounts, along with reminiscences of those who loved or loathed Joseph, give context to the dramatic life of this distinct religionist. Joseph's story is further developed in interviews with noted scholars conducted by Lee Groberg specifically for this project. He provided the archival images as well. We both appreciate the willing support of the Marriott Foundation, whose sponsorship gave life to this whole project.

The portrait of Joseph Smith on the cover of this book was commissioned specifically for this volume. Painted by Del Parson in 1998, it reflects descriptions of Joseph from journals and commentaries of his time. I see it as Joseph in Nauvoo: bold and determined.

More than a hundred images of the Prophet Joseph can be found today in archives and private collections. The Church of Jesus Christ of Latter-day Saints and the Reorganized Church of Jesus Christ of Latter Day Saints offer rich resources in likenesses, though a caution from Rachel Ridgeway Grant, who knew Joseph Smith in Nauvoo, is worth noting, "There are some pictures that do not look, a particle like him."[2]

Perhaps some of his magic was his striking personality and appearance. He "looked the soul and honor of integrity,"[3] according to Bathsheba W. Smith. "The Prophet was a handsome man,—splendid looking, a large man, tall and fair and his hair was light," she said. "He had a very nice complexion, his eyes were blue, and his hair a golden brown."[4] A reporter from the *St. Louis Weekly Gazette* suggested that "the Prophet's most remarkable feature [was] his eye."[5]

He "stood an even six feet high in his stocking feet and weighed 212 pounds,"[6] according to his cousin John L. Smith. "Altogether he presented a very formidable appearance, being a man of gentlemanly bearing,"[7] James Palmer concluded. "Saints and sinners alike felt and recognized a power and influence which he carried with him,"[8] asserted Mary Alice Cannon Lambert. A congressman who heard Joseph Smith speak in Washington reported to his wife, "He is . . . what you ladies would call a very good-looking man."[9]

Joseph was indeed a powerful presence in New York, Ohio, Missouri, and Illinois. John M. Chidester, upon meeting the Prophet, announced that he had "stood face to face with the greatest man on earth."[10] Mary Elizabeth Rollins Lightner recalled that the first time she met the Prophet Joseph, "He looked at me so earnestly I felt almost afraid, and I thought, 'He can read my every thought.'"[11] A reporter from the *Boston Bee* registered surprise at the Joseph he met in Nauvoo: "I could not help noticing that he dressed, talked and acted like other men, and in every respect appeared exactly the opposite of what I had conjured up in my imagination a prophet [to be]."[12]

Dr. Carol Madsen of the Smith Institute at Brigham Young University explains, "As I read diary after diary, I find that the most pervasive emotion that is expressed about Joseph Smith is

one of gratitude, that somehow they were in the right place at the right time, heard the gospel of the restored church, and were blessed to be able to part of that."[13]

I, too, feel gratitude for the richness of all those who have contributed to this work on Joseph Smith. Sheri Dew, Shadow Mountain vice president of publishing and a dear friend, was an early, steady, and thoughtful force in bringing this book together. Kent Ware, director of publishing, steered the course with polish and such kindness; Emily Watts, editor, was generous, patient, brilliant, and always my champion. Special thanks also to Elsha Ulberg, administrative assistant, and Patricia Parkinson, typographer, for their helping hands.

Scott Eggers crafted the dramatic design—fitting of a prophet—that gives expression and elaboration to Joseph's story. John Snyder followed Joseph's footsteps across America, shooting color photographs that speak with compelling character from the pages. Dennis Millard's digital design craftsmanship added significantly to the emotion of the imagery. Lauri Eskelson's production stills from the documentary were important contributions.

Dr. Craig Manscill acted as historical consultant, giving keen perspective; religion professor Cal Stevens read carefully the final manuscript. Margaret Smoot became for me a much-needed extra pair of eyes.

To all the historians, archivists, writers, and researchers who for years have studied Mormonism and the Prophet Joseph, thank you for your diligence and exacting efforts. I pay particular tribute to Dr. Leonard J. Arrington, who time and again gave insights and a listening ear. And to his wife, my mother, Harriet, my thank you for her ever-present good heart.

Most of all, thanks and gratitude go to the Swinton family, my husband, Jeffrey, in particular. Constant in his encouragement, frank in his review, chipper and ever able to shoulder the burdens of a writer-wife, he is my greatest strength and deserves a standing ovation, as do our children, Ian, Jonathan, Daniel, and Cameron and his wife, Kristen.

With fullness of heart, I also thank Joseph Smith. In 1828 Oliver Cowdery received what he considered an admonition from the Lord to "stand by my servant Joseph." I, like Oliver, have taken that counsel to heart and have counted it an honor and sacred trust to be in the company of the American Prophet.

Heidi S. Swinton
Salt Lake City, Utah

AUTHORITIES CITED

Following are the names and professional affiliations of those people interviewed in connection with the PBS documentary American Prophet: The Story of Joseph Smith *who are quoted in this companion book. Quotations from them that appear in this volume were all selected from the transcripts of those interviews.*

DR. LEONARD J. ARRINGTON
Former Church Historian
The Church of Jesus Christ
of Latter-day Saints

ELDER M. RUSSELL BALLARD
The Church of Jesus Christ
of Latter-day Saints

DR. RICHARD L. BUSHMAN
Professor of History
Columbia University

DR. MARIO DEPILLIS
Professor Emeritus,
American Social and
Religious History
Amherst College

DR. RONALD K. ESPLIN
Director,
Joseph Fielding Smith
Institute for Church History
Brigham Young University

DR. NATHAN HATCH
Provost
University of Notre Dame

PRESIDENT GORDON B.
HINCKLEY
The Church of Jesus Christ
of Latter-day Saints

DR. RICHARD T. HUGHES
Professor of Religion
Pepperdine University

ELAINE L. JACK
Former Relief Society
General President
The Church of Jesus Christ
of Latter-day Saints

DR. CAROL MADSEN
Professor,
Joseph Fielding Smith
Institute for Church History
Brigham Young University

DR. MARTIN E. MARTY
Professor and Director,
Public Religion Project
The University of Chicago
Divinity School

DR. W. GRANT MCMURRAY
Historian
Reorganized Church of
Jesus Christ of Latter Day
Saints

DR. ROBERT MILLET
Dean of Religious
Education
Brigham Young University

DR. LARRY MOORE
Professor of History
Cornell University

ELDER DALLIN H. OAKS
The Church of Jesus Christ
of Latter-day Saints

DR. ROSS PETERSON
Professor of History
Utah State University

DR. ROBERT REMINI
Historian
University of Illinois at
Chicago

DR. JAN SHIPPS
Professor Emeritus, History
of American Religion
Indiana University—Purdue
University, Indianapolis
(IUPUI)

DR. DAVID WHITTAKER
Special Collections, Harold
B. Lee Library
Brigham Young University

DR. GORDON S. WOOD
Professor of History
Brown University

PROLOGUE

A HOLY WAR, it had raged for years. Joseph Smith and his religious faithful had sought to establish their Zion in one community after another. Not even the wilderness would have them. At the end, there was no battleground but there were prisoners—celebrated ones, at that. ✕✕✕✕✕✕✕✕✕✕✕✕✕✕

IN THE LATE afternoon on June 27, 1844, a mob craving its own frontier form of justice crept across an Illinois pasture and surrounded the jail at Carthage. The militia that had been mustered to keep the peace mounted no resistance. A small pack of the attackers stormed up the stairs and swiftly fired shots into the second-floor cell that housed the Mormon prophet, Joseph Smith, his brother Hyrum, and his friends John Taylor and Willard Richards. The melee ended as quickly as it had begun.

A dispatch from Willard Richards to the anxious citizens in nearby Nauvoo reported the grim news: "Joseph and Hyrum are dead. Taylor wounded, not very badly. I am well. Our guard was forced, as we believe, by a band of . . . 100 to 200. The job was done in an instant."[1]

For fourteen years Joseph Smith Jr. had led a religion born on America soil. Though he had built his church on the western frontiers—New York, Ohio, Missouri, and finally Illinois—this American prophet was a phenomenon that attracted national attention. His was more than a religious movement. It was, as described in 1842 by the editor of the *New York Herald*, "a spiritual system, combined also with morals and industry, that may change the destiny of the race."[2]

Joseph explained his sense of mission in 1844: "I intend to lay a foundation that will revolutionize the whole world."[3] That change embraced what he considered was a calling from God to restore the true church, translate records from ancient plates and publish them as new scripture called the Book of Mormon, organize a lay priesthood, build holy temples, and establish "the kingdom of God on earth." Thousands from the New England states, Canada, the East Coast, and the British Isles flocked to the message of Jesus Christ, a restoration of His gospel, and the coming Millennium. Such an orientation challenged religious pluralism and demonstrated people's dissatisfaction with an increasingly sectarian society.

The Mormons took refuge in building a sacred Zion. Their efforts sparked controversy time and again until the fateful days of late June 1844, when the Prophet Joseph was charged with treason and ordered by Illinois Governor Thomas Ford to turn himself in at Carthage, the Hancock County seat.

That community, twenty-five miles southeast of the Mormons' city of Nauvoo, had been agitated for days. Bands of vigilante townsmen and farmers from surrounding areas had been pressing for the arrest of their archenemy, Joseph Smith. When he arrived, the Carthage Greys—the local militia—unruly and decidedly anti-Mormon, were commissioned to keep the peace.

In the days that followed, Joseph was paraded before the troops, brought before a judge, and then locked in Carthage Jail. Eight

"WHILE THERE WERE GUARDS AROUND THE JAIL," EYEWITNESS WILLIAM HAMILTON DECLARED, "THEY WERE GUARDS THAT DID NOT GUARD."[4] OF THE 22,000 RESIDENTS OF HANCOCK COUNTY, HALF WERE MORMONS. CARTHAGE NUMBERED A FEW HUNDRED, WARSAW ABOUT FIVE HUNDRED.

of his friends elected to stay with him. On June 27, a guard at the jail boasted to one of Joseph's companions of the imminent end of the prized prisoner: "We have had too much trouble to bring Old Joe here to let him ever escape alive, and unless you want to die with him you had better leave before sundown . . . and you'll see that I can prophesy better than Old Joe."[5]

That afternoon a mob of men stormed the jail. In a flash they were up the stairs and firing through the door into the room where the prisoners were held. Hyrum Smith fell first, struck in the face. Joseph got off three rounds at the assailants; his gun misfired the other three barrels. A bevy of shots poured into the room from another party of aggressors positioned on the ground outside. John Taylor received several bullets, including one from outside that hit the watch in his vest pocket, stopping it at 5:16 P.M. Willard Richards was grazed but essentially unharmed. Joseph was struck from behind as he ran for the window. He fell to the ground outside, having been hit four times, twice in the back. The fatal incident lasted less than three minutes.

Joseph's younger brother Samuel, fearing for the safety of his older siblings, had saddled his horse and headed for Carthage that afternoon. He arrived to find his brothers dead and the town deserted. Fearing a reprisal from the Mormons, Joseph's foes had fled to the country,

THE RESPONSE
FAITHFUL WAS STU

FROM THE NAUVOO

ED SILENCE.

as had many of the townspeople. From house to house the cry spread, "The Mormons are coming." County officials packed up the county records and moved them to Quincy for safe-keeping. Governor Ford, returning from having delivered a strong rebuke to the Mormons in Nauvoo, made a hasty exit too. The roads heading south and southeast—the opposite direction from the Mormon stronghold—were crowded with both those who had joined in the assault and those who had waited and watched.

Willard Richards's missive to the Mormons had warned, "The citizens here are afraid of the Mormons attacking them. I promise them no![26]

The response from the Nauvoo faithful was stunned silence. While they doubled the watch and fortified their guard stations, Joseph's followers wrestled with a grief they had never known. Lucy Meserve Bean Smith reflected on the mood that horrific night: "On the evening of the 27th of June such a barking and howling of dogs and bellowing of cattle all over the city of Nauvoo I never heard before nor since. . . . I knelt down and tried to pray for the Prophet, but I was struck speechless, and knew not the cause till next morning. Of course the awful deed was already accomplished, when the spirit refused to give me utterance to the prayer the evening before.[27]

The Smiths' cortege left Carthage early the next morning, Friday, June 28. Each wagon carried a grim cargo in a lidless pine box; prairie brush and branches masked the corpses from the summer sun. Richards, flanked by a handful of militia, escorted the wagons home. The procession reached Nauvoo about 3:00 P.M.

A line of mourners had begun to form about two o'clock that afternoon. Men, women, and children, still in shock from the news, waited quietly in the streets for the return of their leader. William Hyde observed, "My soul sickened and I wept before the Lord and for a time it seemed that the very Heavens were clad in mourning."[8]

Said Maria Wealthy Wilcox, "It can be well imagined, the sorrow and darkness that seemed to pervade the whole place."[9] James Madison Fisher described the melancholy, "Everything seamed to turn as black as ink."[10] Aroet Hale, who later played the snare drums at the funeral, said of the sight, "To See Stout men and women Standing around in group[s] Crying & morning for the Loss of their Dear Prophet and Patriarch was Enough to break the hart of a Stone."[11] "The love the saints had for him was inexpressible," said Mary Alice Cannon Lambert. "Oh, the mourning in the land!" she lamented. "The grief felt was beyond expression—men, women and children, we were all stunned by the blow."[12]

AN ESTIMATED ten thousand farmers, laborers, housewives, children, businessmen, newcomers to Nauvoo, leaders of the church, members of the City Council, and officers and volunteers from the Nauvoo Legion thronged the streets. Many of the new converts from Britain, Ireland, and Wales raised a melancholy moan, a keening that could be heard beyond the borders of what was later called the "City of Joseph."

Nearly ten thousand mourners filed through the Mansion House to pay their respects to Joseph and Hyrum.

He had been their townsman, political leader, general, friend, and, in their eyes, an instrument in God's hand to restore the gospel of Jesus Christ and His true church. Jane James, a young black woman who had been employed at the Smith home, described her feelings of loss: "Yes, indeed. I [knew] the Prophet Joseph. That lovely hand! He used to put it out to me. Never passed me without shaking hands with me wherever he was. Oh, he was the finest man I ever saw on earth. . . . When he was killed . . . I could have died, just laid down and died."[13]

Zions noblest sons are weeping;

See her daughters bathed in tears,

Where the prophets now are sleeping,

Nature's sleep—the sleep of years . . .

Joseph and Hyrum were brought in from Carthage to Nauvoo it was Judged by menny boath in and out of the church that there was more then five barels of tears shed. I cannot bare to think enny thing about it."[20]

NOT EVERYONE was saddened by Joseph's death, however. Those who opposed him believed that the Mormons had been held captive by the Prophet's diabolical powers, and if he were gone, the Mormon effort would collapse. The *New York Herald*, for example, predicted: "The death of the modern mahomet will seal the fate of Mormonism. They cannot get another Joe Smith. The holy city must tumble into ruins, and the 'latter-day saints' have indeed come to the latter day."[21]

Rival clergymen were quick to commend the mob action. An exultant Alexander Campbell, whose congregations had been "raided" by Mormon missionaries and who had been vilifying Joseph since his New York days, boldly announced in his *Millennial Harbinger* that the murder was an act of God:

"The money digger, the juggler, and the founder of the Golden Bible delusion, has been hurried away in the midst of his madness to his final account. 'He died not as a righteous man dieth.' The hand of the Lord was heavy upon him. An outlaw himself, God cut him off by outlaws. . . . It was the outrages of the Mormons that brought upon the head of their leader the arm of justice. . . . Religion or religious opinions had nothing to do with it. It was neither more nor less than the assassination of one whose career was in open rebellion against God and man."[22]

Reverend William G. Brownlow of the *Jonesborough Whig* scorned the lamentations being printed by some papers: "Some of the public Journals of the country, we are sorry to see, regret the death of that blasphemous wretch Joe Smith, the Mormon Prophet. Our deliberate judgement is, that he ought to have been dead ten years ago, and that those who at length have deprived him of his life, have done the cause of God, and of the country, good service." Reverend Brownlow did not hide his enthusiasm when he concluded, "Smith was killed, as he should have been. THREE CHEERS to the brave company who shot him to pieces!"[23]

Other accounts were more tempered. The Iowa *Bloomington Herald* said, "Assassins may plunge the dagger to the heart of the innocent

CARTHAGE JAIL

THREE
CHEERS
to THE BRAVE COMPANY WHO
SHOT HIM
TO PIECES!

—REVEREND WILLIAM G. BROWNLOW,
JONESBOROUGH WHIG

and unsuspecting savages may torture, kill and slay, but their crimes are virtues in comparison with the heart of the reputed civilized man who in cold blood murders the victim

I THINK I WOULD SAY THAT FROM 1492 OR 1607 UNTIL NOW, AMERICA HAS NO MATCH FOR JOSEPH SMITH IN THE DRAMA OF FORMING A NEW RELIGIOUS COMMUNITY . . . A NEW RELIGIOUS TRADITION. THERE'S BEEN A LOT OF REVITALIZATION OF THE OLD TRADITIONS. THERE HAVE BEEN SOME SEMISUCCESSFUL AND UNSUCCESSFUL NEW SCRIPTURES AND NEW TRADITIONS. BUT NO ONE MATCHES HIM FOR THE SIX MILLION HEREABOUT AND FOR THE TWELVE AND SOON TWENTY MILLION AROUND THE WORLD WHO KEEP ATTESTING HIM DAY BY DAY AND BUILDING COMMUNITY DAY BY DAY.

—*Dr. Martin Marty, University of Chicago*

who has voluntarily placed himself in the hands of his enemy, to be tried and dealt with according to law."[24]

The *Missouri Republican*, speaking from the state that had brutally expelled the Mormons only a few years before, now sounded a more penitent tone, referring to the killing of the

Smiths as "perfidious, blackhearted, cowardly murder—so wanton as to be without any justification—so inhuman and treacherous as to find no parallel in savage life under any circumstances."[25]

A few newspapers boldly spoke with admiration for this American prophet. The *New York Sun* suggested, "It is no small thing, in the blaze of this nineteenth century, to give to men a new revelation, found a new religion, establish new forms of worship, to build a city, with new laws, institutions, and orders of architecture,—to establish ecclesiastic, civil and military jurisdiction, found colleges, send out missionaries, and make proselytes in two hemispheres: yet all this has been done by Joe Smith, and that against every sort of opposition, ridicule and persecution."[26]

About two weeks after the Carthage incident, the *New York Weekly Herald* reported, "Thus died the plowboy Prophet of America at the hands of an assassin, the object of intense, local persecution within Hancock County, where feeling ran high in the communities of Carthage and Warsaw against Nauvoo, its balance of power and the Prophet. Yet, out beyond the vineyards of Hancock County, beyond that beautiful bend in the Mississippi, he was a respected and an admired Prophet and statesman."[27]

From around the country came messages of support for those with friends and family in Nauvoo. "What earthly power has ever yet stood before the overpowering energies of a religious creed?" queried a highly respected gentleman from Fair Haven, Connecticut, of his friend in Nauvoo. "Indeed, we do not know

JOSEPH WAS AN INCREDIBLE MAN. FOR SOMEONE TO WALK LARGE ON THE STAGE OF HISTORY, AND ACCOMPLISH INCREDIBLE THINGS WITHOUT A REMARKABLE INVENTION, OR AN INHERITED FORTUNE, OR A STROKE OF LUCK OR DISCOVERING SOMETHING IS INCREDIBLE. —ELDER DALLIN H. OAKS, THE CHURCH OF JESUS CHRIST OF LATTER-DAY SAINTS

which has the worst effect on the community, the doctrines of Smith or the ten thousand false rumors constantly put in circulation against him. One thing is certain, his name will survive when those who grossly misrepresent him have become blanks on the page of the future."[28]

Governor Ford later noted in his *History of Illinois*, "Upon the principle that 'the blood of the martyrs is the seed of the church', there was now really more cause than ever to predict its success. The murder of the Smiths, instead of putting an end to the delusion of the Mormons and dispersing them, as many believed it would, only bound them together closer than ever, gave them new confidence in their faith and an increased fanaticism."[29]

Weeks before his death, the Prophet Joseph was visited by Josiah Quincy, soon to become mayor of Boston, Massachusetts. Years later, in his book *Figures of the Past*, Quincy judged Joseph Smith to be a force of surprising significance:

"It is by no means improbable that some future textbook, for the use of generations yet unborn, will contain a question something like this: What historical American of the nineteenth century has exerted the most powerful influence upon the destinies of his countrymen? And it is by no means impossible that the answer to that interrogatory may be thus written: *Joseph Smith, the Mormon Prophet*. And the reply, absurd as it doubtless seems to most men now living, may be an obvious commonplace to their descendants."[30]

Joseph Smith is obviously the most successful American prophet that we've ever had. He established a religion that has not only lasted but flourished and grown to become the most powerful, uniquely American religion that we've ever had.

–DR. GORDON WOOD, BROWN UNIVERSITY

FROM THESE ROOTS

1

AMERICA: the land of the bold, the believing. The land of promise. For centuries this country has beckoned to those "yearning to breathe free," and they have come. From these roots rose Joseph Smith Jr., American prophet.

JOSEPH SMITH was American in his heritage and in his style as well. A rugged individualist, he defied convention. His seeming religious crusade antagonized many; they saw him as "sinful and errant."[1] Opposition dogged him all his days, yet he was driven by what he said was "a work that God and angels have contemplated with delight for generations past; that fired the souls of the ancient patriarchs and prophets."[2]

Set in the first half of the nineteenth century, his story chronicles more than an episode in this nation's religious experience. It is a saga of a people and their prophet that calls to mind the rights of all Americans to worship how, when, and where they please. That desire has tugged at the hearts of mankind through the ages.

In its varied faces and forms, religion has been at home in this land—though the pursuit of it has not always been easy. Freedom of religion attracted many of the early colonizers to the New World. They brought with them reformed images of worship that had washed across the European continent and now found harbor in the newly settled villages dotting the Atlantic coast. In the years that followed, a complex society emerged, one that recognized the traditions of established religion yet made place for the non-churched, accepted the skeptics yet opened the door for new divination of truth.

The Mayflower Compact, the first of several defining documents, clearly articulated that settlement was for the "advancement of the Christian faith." Increase Mather, president of Harvard College and noted religious scholar, reportedly described the colonies' emerging identity, "There never was a generation that did not perfectly shake off the dust of Babylon, both as to ecclesiastical and civil constitution, as the first generation of Christians that came to this land for the Gospel's sake."[3]

In the Revolutionary War era, the Founding Fathers crafted further definition. These were God-fearing statesmen of a new nation, one with an already uncommon identity. The Constitution

The Latter-day Saint story has to be in the top five story fascinations in American religious history. Mormonism is America's most rooted religion. Joseph Smith's great contribution is capturing a version of the American story and projecting it into the future. —DR. MARTIN MARTY, UNIVERSITY OF CHICAGO

GOD GOVERNS IN THE AFFAIRS OF MEN!
WITHOUT HIS CONCURRING AID, WE SHALL
SUCCEED IN THIS POLITICAL BUILDING NO
BETTER THAN THE BUILDERS OF BABEL.

—Benjamin Franklin

of the United States, they maintained, was designed for a moral and religious people. "God governs in the affairs of Men!" announced Benjamin Franklin. "Without His concurring aid, we shall succeed in this political building no better than the builders of Babel."[4]

IT WAS A PERIOD IN WHICH I BELIEVE THE AMERICAN TYPE AS WE KNOW IT TODAY FINALLY EVOLVED OUT OF A COLONIAL EUROPEAN SOCIETY. THERE WERE EXTRAORDINARY CHANGES TAKING PLACE. A NATIONALISM HAD RISEN. A MARKET REVOLUTION WAS PUT IN PLACE. WE DEVELOPED AN INDEPENDENT NATIONAL ECONOMY. WE MOVED WESTWARD ACROSS A FRONTIER, A CONTINENT THAT STRETCHED THREE THOUSAND MILES. AND THERE WERE POLITICAL CHANGES OF GREAT IMPORTANCE. THE DEVELOPMENT OF DEMOCRACY, THE SOCIAL REFORMS THAT WERE PUT IN PLACE REMADE THE COUNTRY. TALK ABOUT FUTURE SHOCK FOR THESE PEOPLE. ALL OF A SUDDEN THEY HAD A NEW COUNTRY. ALL OF A SUDDEN THEY WERE BUILDING A NEW SOCIETY IN EVERY WAY.

—Dr. Robert Remini, University of Illinois at Chicago

America produced more religions in the period from 1790 to 1860 than any other segment of western culture. Congregationalists, Episcopalians, and Presbyterians had dominated during the mid-1700s, but in the 1800s, the Baptists and Methodists began to draw great numbers, as did Quakers, Shakers, and Universalists. That splintering continued as people moved west and families were distanced from the religions of their fathers.

Despite the burst of church affiliations, those whose devotions questioned the established order were sometimes shunned, discredited, even mobbed and stoned. Faith and fellowship in some communities contrasted with plummeting church attendance in others. Many Americans received religion in their hearts but not necessarily in the pews.

People were trying to make sense of the shifting all around them. Movement from one church to another, one community to another, one vocation to another separated families and shaped a new culture with a new set of needs. "There was a great sense that no matter who

As towns sprang up on the frontier, churches were among the first structures completed by early settlers.

you were or where you came from, you started," says Dr. Martin Marty. "You might homestead. You might get your property. And you might clear a woods, and you might found a town. And when you did, you had to ask the basic questions of life. Who am I? Am I called to do this? Who's calling me? Am I respon-sible? Am I a steward of something that's given me undeserved? Am I an achiever? And that's

made the Americans an extremely religious, spiritually energetic people."[5]

To this new social order came Joseph Smith Jr. Born in Sharon, Vermont, he was a fifth-generation American. His mother, Lucy Mack Smith, wrote of his birth, "We had a son whom we called Joseph after the name of his father; he was born December 23, 1805."[6]

Joseph came from hearty New England stock. His paternal ancestor Robert Smith left Kirton, England, for the colonies in 1638, settling in Topsfield, Massachusetts. The Smiths became sig-nificant contributors to their community and their country. Smiths fought in the Revolutionary War, served in elected office, and held a pew in the Congregationalist Church. Joseph's great-grandfather Samuel, a Revolutionary War hero, was heralded at his death in November 1785 for his citizenship and his religious conviction: "[He] was esteemed a man of integrity and uprightness . . . a sincere friend

PARENTS
Joseph Smith, Sr. 1771-1840
Lucy Mack 1775-1856

PATERNAL GRANDPARENTS
Asael Smith 1744-1830
Mary Duty 1743-1836

MATERNAL GRANDPARENTS
Solomon Mack 1732-1820
Lydia Gates 1732-c.1818

PATERNAL GREAT GRANDPARENTS
Samuel Smith 1714-1785
Priscilla Gould 1707-1744

MATERNAL GREAT GRANDPARENTS
Ebenezer Mack 1697-1777
Hannah Huntley 1708-1796

PATERNAL GREAT GRANDPARENTS
Moses Duty 1700-1778
Mary Palmer 1717-c.1791

MATERNAL GREAT GRANDPARENTS
Daniel Gates 1707-1775
Lydia Fuller 1709-1778

to the liberties of his country, and a strenuous advocate for the doctrines of Christianity."[7]

Asael Smith, Joseph's grandfather, predicted that God would raise up some branch of the Smiths to be a great benefit to mankind. A God-fearing man, Asael wrote in a last epistle to his family, "Do all to God in a serious manner. . . . And as to religion, . . . study the nature of religion, and see whether it consists in outward for-

malities, or in the hidden man of the heart." He affirmed his own beliefs with, "Sure am I, my Savior, Christ, is perfect, and never will fail."[8]

Joseph's maternal ancestors, the Macks, were Scottish, some of them clergy. His grandfather Solomon, a good-hearted Christian, played out most of his life in a succession of failed business prospects and military enlistments. He finally found religion and became an ardent missionary, admonishing his family to bring up their children in fear of the Lord.

Of Joseph Smith's lineage, Brigham Young, second president of The Church of Jesus Christ of Latter-day Saints, said: "It was decreed in the counsels of eternity, long before the foundations of the earth were laid, that he [Joseph Smith] should be the man, in the last dispensation of this world, to bring forth the word of God to the people, and receive the fulness of the keys and power of the Priesthood of the Son of God. The Lord had his eye upon him, and upon his father, and upon his father's father, and upon their progenitors clear back to Abraham, and from Abraham to the flood, from the flood to Enoch, and from Enoch to Adam. He has watched that family and that blood as it has circulated from its fountain to the birth of that man."[9]

Joseph was "remarkably quiet, well-disposed,"[10] reported his mother of his early years. He was the fourth of nine children, and his childhood was marked by a succession of moves as his father sought to make a living in the New England hills. In other respects his

"As to religion ... see whether it consists in outward formalities, or in the hidden man of the heart."

youth was, for the most part, uneventful. "Nothing occurred during his early life except those trivial circumstances which are common to that state of human existence,"[11] wrote his mother.

The Smiths were living in West Lebanon, New Hampshire, when an epidemic of typhoid fever attacked the community. Seven-year-old Joseph was sick for two weeks and seemingly recovered, but then developed complications that showed first as an abscess in his shoulder and then as an agonizing pain in his leg. His older brother Hyrum "sat beside him, almost day and night for some considerable length of time," his mother later wrote, "holding the affected part of [Joseph's] leg in his hands and pressing it between them, so that his afflicted brother might be enabled to endure the pain which was so excruciating that he was scarcely able to bear it."[12]

After two weeks a doctor from nearby Dartmouth College recommended amputating Joseph's leg. When the Smiths would not consent, the doctor performed instead a new procedure, cutting away only the infected portion of the bone. Joseph's father held the young boy in his arms for the operation; Joseph had refused to take brandy to dull the pain. "The Lord will help me, and I shall get through it," he announced.[13] Joseph survived the ordeal, though he walked for three years with crutches and showed signs of a slight limp the rest of his life.

The Smiths farmed the wooded hills of Vermont. They were poor. A series of unseasonable frosts, caused by a massive volcanic eruption in 1815 in Indonesia, wrought havoc on the growing season in America. In 1816, after three crop failures in a row, the Smiths packed up and went west to the Finger Lakes

The Smith family, moving fro[m]
Very, very hard. Very margina[l]
ing a move would increase their fortune[s]
dream sort of eluded them in the lifetim[e]

[WE] WERE ... SUPPORT OF A LARGE

—JOSEPH SMITH

district of upstate New York, where the soil was reported to be rich and easily tilled.

The family arrived in the new area nearly penniless, "not from indolence, but on account of many reverses of fortune, with which our lives had been rather singularly marked,"[14] Lucy wrote.

"Being in indigent circumstances [we] were obliged to labour hard for the support of a large family having nine children," recalled Joseph in later years. "Therefore we were deprived of the bennifit of an education suffice it to say I was merely instructed in reading writing and the ground rules of Arithmetic which constituted my whole literary acquirements."[15]

Most Americans before the Civil War tended to depend for their livelihood upon agriculture or agriculture-related occupations. It was heavy labor. Their lives were pretty much determined by the cycles of the year: planting, harvesting, and so forth. That meant schooling for children was for the most part limited to the winter season, when the crops were in and snows or bad weather prevented working in the fields. But it was a very physically demanding occupation. Most of their clothes and day-to-day utensils were either handmade or acquired by bartering with neighbors.

Palmyra was a community with promise. Its proximity to the Erie Canal, under construction in 1825, boded well for its future as an agricultural and commercial center. The Smiths hoped to share in that prosperity.

Vermont westward into New York, clearly reflected that lifestyle.

s it turns out. They were always wanting to do better and often think-

nd their opportunities. As it turned out for the Smith family, that

f Joseph Smith's father. —DR. DAVID WHITTAKER, BRIGHAM YOUNG UNIVERSITY

LO HERE, LO THERE

2

WESTERN New York was so fired up with religious talk in the early decades of the nineteenth century that historians later dubbed it "the burned-over district." Camps, revivals, street corners, and Sunday meetings were ablaze with believers pushing orthodoxy aside for a more experiential form of worship, something they could take into their own hands and hearts. ✕✕✕✕✕✕✕✕✕✕✕✕✕

OUNTLESS revivalists and reformers preached of the road to repentance and salvation. Spirited services were repeated night after night. Churches extended the prospect of salvation and the promise of peace. With great zeal the people sought spiritual signs, grace, glory, and God. They debated the Bible, the nature of Deity, life beyond the grave, baptism, priesthood authority, and the second coming of Jesus Christ. Those caught up in this "hotbed of evangelical preaching"[1] were called "seekers."

The Smiths were among those who sounded the theme, "What must I do to be saved?" Joseph Smith Sr. had dreams that to him affirmed Joel's promise in the Bible, "your old men shall dream dreams, your young men shall see visions" (Joel 2:28). Lucy had her own spiritual yearnings, "I cried out, in the agony of my soul, 'Oh, Lord God, I beseech thee, in the name of Jesus Christ, to forgive my sins.'"[2]

Both were focused on the religious training of their family. With their children they studied the Bible, sang hymns, and gathered for morning and evening prayers.

Young Joseph "seemed much less inclined to the perusal of good books than any of the rest of our children," reported his mother. He was "far more given to meditation and deep study."[3] He also manifested a deep awareness of his own spiritual condition, saying, "My mind became seriously imprest with regard to the all important concerns for the well-fare of my immortal Soul."[4]

All about him he found confusion. He later wrote, "Great multitudes united themselves to the different religious parties, which created no small stir and division amongst the people, some crying, 'Lo here!' and others, 'Lo there!'"[5] Yet he was determined to find answers.

"I knew not who was right or who was wrong," he wrote, "and I considered it of the first importance that I should be right, in matters that involve eternal consequences."[6]

Questioning abounded, which prompted a local religious leader, Reverend William Bacon, to caution, "If you embrace wrong doctrines and unite with a corrupt church, you may expect coldness and darkness all your lives."[7] Competition for souls allowed little tolerance for other persuasions.

Joseph's mother, Lucy, brothers Hyrum and Samuel, and sister Sophronia joined the Presbyterian faith. His father remained uncommitted, his leanings to the broad context offered by the Universalists. But Joseph was uncertain. He saw religious leaders "adorn their profession by a holy walk and Godly conversation" but did not find a "society or denomination that built upon the gospel of Jesus Christ."[8] He was thoughtful "concerning

Some people would describe

the number of religious options

as deafening. You would hear one preacher

one day, you'd hear another preacher the next.

—DR. NATHAN HATCH, UNIVERSITY OF NOTRE DAME

the situation of the world of mankind, the contentions and divisions, the wickedness and abominations and the darkness which pervaded the minds of mankind."[9] For a period he stopped attending church and camp meetings altogether, explaining to his mother, "I can take my Bible, and go into the woods, and

I often said to myself, what is to be done? Who of all these parties are right; Or are they all wrong together? —JOSEPH SMITH

learn more in two hours, than you can learn at meeting in two years."[10]

Joseph later described his quandary: "In the midst of this war of words, and tumult of opinions, I often said to myself, what is to be done? Who of all these parties are right? Or are they all wrong together? And if any one of them be right which is it? And how shall I know it?"[11]

He took to heart a scripture from the New Testament epistle of James: "If any of you lack wisdom, let him ask of God, that giveth to all men liberally, and upbraideth not; and it shall be given him."[13] Said Joseph of that promise, "Never did any passage of scripture come with more power to the heart of man that this did at this time to mine . . . knowing that if any person needed wisdom from God, I did."[13]

On a spring day in 1820, fourteen-year-old Joseph went to the woods near his home to pray. "Having looked around me and finding myself alone, I kneeled down and began to offer up the desires of my heart to God."[14] He later said of the experience, "I was seized upon by some power which entirely overcame me. . . . Thick darkness gathered around me and it seemed to me for a time as if I were doomed to sudden destruction."[15]

At "this moment of great alarm," he wrote, "[I exerted] all my powers to call upon God to deliver me out of the power of this enemy."[16]

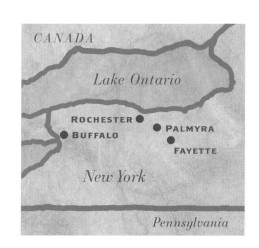

What followed was what would come to be known to his followers as Joseph Smith's First Vision: "I saw a pillar of light exactly over my head above the brightness of the sun, which descended gradually untill it fell upon me. . . . When the light rested upon me I saw two personages (whose brightness and glory defy all description) standing above me in the air. One of them spake unto me calling me by name and said (pointing to the other) This is My Beloved Son, Hear Him!"[17]

Joseph asked the personages which of the religions he should join. According to his account, "They told me that all religious denominations were believing in incorrect doctrines, and that none of them was acknowledged of God as his church and kingdom." Said Joseph, "I was expressly commanded to 'go not after them,' at the same time receiving a promise that the fulness of the gospel should at some future time be made known unto me."[18]

Days later, Joseph confided to a local minister that he had seen a vision. "I was greatly surprised at his behaviour," he said. "He treated my communication not only lightly but with great contempt, saying it was all of the Devil, that there were no such things as visions or revelations in these days, that all such things had ceased with the apostles and that there never would be any more of them."[19] That disdain was shared by others who heard of the young lad's experience. Those who professed

He walked down to the grove of trees where he could be all by himself, and there knelt and offered up prayer asking for wisdom concerning the course he should take. And out of that inquiry came this glorious manifestation of the Father and the Son. It was so meaningful. He learned that the Father and the resurrected Lord are tangible beings of substance and form. That they can speak. . . . It changed the whole picture. Out of that one experience came a new and vital and convincing and moving description of Deity.

—*President Gordon B. Hinckley, The Church of Jesus Christ of Latter-day Saints*

IF ANY OF YOU LACK WISDOM,

LET HIM ASK OF GOD,

THAT GIVETH TO ALL MEN LIBERALLY,

AND UPBRAIDETH NOT:

AND IT SHALL BE GIVEN HIM.

JAMES 1:5

to be teachers of religion attacked Joseph with "the bitterest persecution and reviling."[20]

For the rest of his life, despite constant opposition, Joseph was resolute when he spoke of his experience. "I had actualy seen a light and in the midst of that light I saw two personages, and they did in reality speak to me." The clamor against him never did end, and he said, "Though I was hated and persecuted for saying that I had seen a vision, yet it was true."[21] Time and again Joseph repeated his portrayal of his singular visitation, "I knew it, and I knew that God knew it, and I could not deny it."[22]

Whereas he had once been courted by assorted clergymen, Joseph was now the subject of ridicule and derision. Confused by the

---

I AM ABSOLUTELY CONVINCED THAT HE DESCRIBED A VISION. AND WHEN VISIONS ARE DESCRIBED, IT IS NOT UP TO OUTSIDERS TO SAY THAT COULDN'T HAVE HAPPENED. —*Dr. Jan Shipps, Indiana University*

---

outrage and distortions, he said, "Though I was an obscure boy only between fourteen and fifteen years of age, and my circumstances in life such as to make a boy of no consequence in the world, yet men of high standing would take notice sufficient to excite the public mind against me and create a hot persecution."[23] As

Elder Dallin H. Oaks of The Church of Jesus Christ of Latter-day Saints explains, "For religious leaders of the day to have a young man say that he had seen the Father and the Son and to reflect on the fact that they had degrees and experience and a calling according to their understanding, and the Lord hadn't spoken to them, well, the words *jealousy* and *envy* and *threat* and *resentment* come quickly to mind."[24]

Taunts and slurs were not the only threats to the young Joseph. "He was out one evening on an errand, and, on returning home, as he was passing through the dooryard, a gun was fired across his pathway with the evident intention of shooting him. He sprang to the door much frightened." The family went in search of the gunman, but could find no trace. They did find an impression in the dirt under a wagon where the assailant had hidden. The balls discharged from the gun lodged in the head and neck of a cow that was standing in the line of fire.[25]

Attacks "at the hand of all classes of men, both religious and irreligious"[26] would become Joseph's constant companions. Later in his ministry he would attest, "Wherever light shone, it stirred up darkness."[27]

Over the next few years, Joseph became concerned with his own behavior, reporting, "I frequently fell into many foolish errors and displayed the weakness of youth, and the foibles of human nature." In making this confession, Joseph explained, "No one need suppose me guilty of any great or malignant sins." But he did admit to being "guilty of levity, and sometimes associated with jovial company, not consistent with that character which ought to be maintained by one who was called of God as I had been."[28]

"When I first looked upon him I was afraid, but the fear soon left me," said Joseph. "He called me by name and said unto me that he was a messenger sent from the presence of God to me." Moroni then explained "that God had a work for me to do, and that my [name]

Wherever light shone, it stirred up darkness. —Joseph Smith

He reported that on September 21, 1823, a Sunday night, he prayed for forgiveness of his sins and follies and "for a manifestation to me that I might know of my state and standing before him."[29] What followed would shape the direction and focus of his life.

"I discovered a light appearing in the room which continued to increase untill the room was lighter than at noonday," recounted Joseph. "Immediately a personage appeared at my bedside standing in the air for his feet did not touch the floor." He described the being as "glorious beyond description . . . his countenance truly like lightning."[30] Joseph said the personage's name was Moroni.

should be had for good and evil among all nations kindreds and tongues."[31]

The angelic messenger spoke of a book engraved on gold plates that contained an account of the former inhabitants of the American continent and a fullness of the everlasting gospel of Jesus Christ. If Joseph were faithful, he would help bring that record to light. Joseph related that twice more during the night the same angel returned to his bedside to reaffirm the message.

That morning following Moroni's visits, Joseph went to work in the fields, but his strength was spent. His father "discovered something to be wrong" and sent Joseph home.

But his trek was interrupted by the angel, who this time directed the seventeen-year-old to tell his father "of the vision and commandments [he] had received." His father expressed no skepticism; he declared, "It was of God."[32] The senior Smith instructed his son to do as the messenger had commanded.

The site where the records were buried was a drumlin hill not far from Joseph's home. There, according to a later statement, he was shown the plates for the first time. They were lying in a stone box that was buried under a rock. He was kept from taking them by Moroni, who made it clear that he was not yet to have the plates.

According to Elder M. Russell Ballard of The Church of Jesus Christ of Latter-day Saints, "Moroni is a great prophet who lived in the Americas. And he is the last prophet in the Americas to ever have in his possession the gold plates upon which was recorded their history and the dealing of our Father in Heaven with the people that lived here in the Americas. It was Moroni that placed those records in the Hill Cumorah. And it's logical and very understandable that when the time came for that record—which is the Book of Mormon, another testament of Jesus Christ—to come forth, that Moroni would be commissioned and sent by the Lord to Joseph Smith."[33]

Four years would pass before Joseph would be allowed to collect the gold plates, though he visited the site where they were buried every year for further tutoring from the messenger Moroni. Joseph described the meetings: "At each time I found the same messenger there and received instruction and intelligence from him." In those sessions Joseph said he learned "what the Lord was going to do, and how and in what manner his kingdom was to be conducted in the last days."[34] On a dozen or more

> DO I PERSONALLY BELIEVE? *No. He may have believed that he did. But whether he saw, I have no evidence for that. And as a historian I must base my conclusion on that. And since I'm not a Mormon who by an act of faith believes it, even though it can't be proved, I have to then make a judgment on the basis of the evidence. However, you can say, look what he did. Is one human being capable of doing this? Without divine help and intervention?* —DR. ROBERT REMINI, UNIVERSITY OF ILLINOIS AT CHICAGO

NOBODY CAN SEAL THE HEAVENS BUT GOD. *If God wants to speak to His children, He can speak to them. And how does God speak to His children? He sends those whom He has commissioned to come and teach. We don't have the right to say he can't talk to His children. . . . He can do it any time he wants to. So be it.*
—ELDER M. RUSSELL BALLARD, THE CHURCH OF JESUS CHRIST OF LATTER-DAY SAINTS

occasions in the coming years Joseph would speak of being chastened, comforted, and instructed by Moroni. And for the rest of his life, he would describe repeated visits from angels and prophets of old.

The Smiths were a close family; they stood by Joseph and his account. His mother wrote, "The ensuing evening, when the family were [all together], Joseph made known to them all that he had communicated to his father in the field, and also of his finding the record, as well as what passed between him and the angel while he was at the place where the plates were deposited."[35] According to his mother, the angel told him "that he could not take them from the place wherein they were deposited until he had learned to keep the commandments of God— not only till he was willing but able to do it."[36]

His younger brother William recalled, "We all had the most implicit confidence in what he said. He was a truthful boy. Father and Mother believed him, why should not the children?"[37]

Joseph continued to share his experiences and his new knowledge with his family. "During our evening conversations, Joseph would occasionally give us some of the most amusing recitals that could be imagined," wrote his mother of that period. "He would describe the ancient inhabitants of this continent, their dress, mode of traveling, and the animals upon which they rode; their cities, their buildings, with every particular; their mode of warfare; and also their religious worship. This he would do with as much ease, seemingly, as if he had spent his whole life among them."[38] Each evening, the attentive family "presented an aspect as singular as any that ever lived upon the face of the earth—all seated in a circle, father, mother, sons and daughters and giving the most profound attention to a boy, eighteen years of age, who had never read the Bible through in his life."[39]

That family circle would be broken in just a few months, when Joseph's oldest brother, Alvin, died in November 1823. His last words were that Joseph must "do everything in his power to obtain the Record."[40]

Alvin's contributions to the family's livelihood had been significant. Extra pressure to help support the family now fell on Joseph and Hyrum, so when landowner and speculator Josiah Stowell offered to hire Joseph in November 1825, he accepted. The job was to search for Spanish treasure across the New York border in Harmony, Pennsylvania.

*T*HERE ARE TIMES IN A PROPHETIC RESTORATION, WHEN THE LORD APPARENTLY WANTS A PURE VESSEL, LIKE THE BOY SAMUEL, OR YOUNG DANIEL, OR JEREMIAH. THEN THE LORD CAN REVEAL HIS MESSAGE TO HIS PEOPLE ON A CLEAN SLATE.

—Elder Dallin H. Oaks,
The Church of Jesus Christ of Latter-day Saints

After weeks of digging, Joseph persuaded Stowell to give up the search. But the quest in the foothills near Harmony was not without reward. While boarding at the home of Isaac Hale, a respected hunter and hard-working Christian, Joseph met and fell in love with his landlord's daughter Emma. The sixth child and third daughter of the Hales, Emma was a schoolteacher. She was dark-haired and hazel-eyed, and stood about five feet nine inches tall. To Joseph she would become "undaunted, firm, and unwavering, unchangeable, affectionate Emma!"[41]

Isaac viewed Joseph as a "careless young man, not very well educated." He had other plans for his daughter. "Young Smith . . . asked my consent to his marrying my daughter Emma," he recorded. "This I refused, and gave him my reasons for so doing; some of which were, that he was a stranger, and followed a business that I could not approve."[42] But Joseph persisted.

"I had no intention of marrying," Emma later wrote of that time. But, "[Joseph] urged me to marry him, and preferring to marry him to any other man I knew, I consented."[43] The two eloped January 18, 1827, and moved in with Joseph's parents in New York. Joseph was twenty-one; Emma was twenty-two.

Eight months later, on September 22, they borrowed a rig, slipped into the night, and headed for the Hill Cumorah, just three miles from the Smith family home. Here, Joseph finally obtained the gold plates containing the ancient records and promptly hid them in a hollow log. The young couple returned home before sunrise.

The gold plates were buried in the Hill Cumorah, just three miles from the Smith family home.

3

JOSEPH SMITH held no rank in the religious society of his hometown. His claims of having received ancient records from a heavenly messenger were met with contempt, if not outright alarm. But a small circle of family and friends believed him. They believed he was called of God. ✕✕✕✕✕✕✕✕✕

JOSEPH KNIGHT, a farmer from Colesville, New York, who had employed Joseph earlier in Harmony, recalled that Joseph had spoken of being told by the angel that "if he would Do right according to the will of God, he mite obtain [the plates] the 22nt day of September Next and if not he never would have them."[1] Knight came to the Smith farm on that designated day. It was his wagon and team that Joseph and Emma borrowed for their late-night rendezvous with Moroni.

When they returned, Joseph was quick to offer, "Do not be uneasy mother, all is right."[2] Because the angel had told him to show the plates to no one, he hid them in a hollow log instead of bringing them home. Joseph was further cautioned, "You will have to be watchful and faithful to your trust, or you will be overpowered by wicked men; for they will lay every plan and scheme that is possible to get it away from you, and if you do not take heed continually, they will succeed."[3]

Joseph described the records, which he said weighed between forty and fifty pounds, as "engraven on plates which had the appearance of gold, each plate was six inches wide and eight inches long, and not quite as thick as common tin. They were filled with engravings, in Egyptian characters and bound together in a volume, as the leaves of a book with three rings running through the whole. The volume was something near six inches in thickness. . . . The whole book exhibited many marks of antiquity in its construction and much skill in the art of engraving."[4]

With the plates was found "a curious instrument," which Joseph called the Urim and Thummim, consisting of "two transparent stones set in the rim of a bow fastened to a breastplate."[5] His mother described the bow as resembling "old-fashioned spectacles."[6]

THE FACT THAT THERE WERE SO MANY RELIGIOUS VOICES WAS VERY BEWILDERING, I THINK, FOR COMMON PEOPLE. AND SO THERE WAS THIS DEEP QUESTIONING, WHAT COULD ONE BELIEVE? AND I THINK THAT'S WHERE THE VOICE OF JOSEPH SMITH DID BECOME A VERY CERTAIN TRUMPET.

WHAT HE SAID IS THAT HE HAD A NEW WORD FROM THE LORD, A NEW KIND OF REVELATION, WHICH WAS CERTAIN AND SURE. IT WAS THE MIRACULOUS INTERVENTION IN MODERN TIMES, JUST AS CHRIST HAD COME IN THE TIME OF THE NEW TESTAMENT. AND THAT MADE GREAT SENSE TO A LOT OF PEOPLE, THAT AMIDST THIS CACOPHONY OF VOICES YOU HAD A CERTAIN TRUMPET THAT OFFERED THE REALITY OF THE SUPERNATURAL TODAY. —Dr. Nathan Hatch, University of Notre Dame

"Each plate was six inches wide and eight inches long, and not quite as thick as common tin."

Though he had hoped to keep word of the records quiet, Joseph had not escaped his neighbors' scrutiny. A frenzied rumor raced through the community that he had gold plates. Joseph Knight said: "People came in to see them. But he told them that they could not for he must not show them."[7] Treasure seekers tried to make a case that they had rights to the plates. Many persisted, offering money and

*J*oseph and Emma moved from New York to this two-room home in Harmony, Pennsylvania. (Structures on left and right were added later.) ➤

property to see them. Said one member of a group plotting to find the plates, "I am not afraid of anybody—we will have them plates in spite of Joe Smith or all the devils in hell."[8]

To protect them, Joseph moved the plates from one hiding place to another. When he first retrieved them from their hiding spot in the woods, he wrapped them in his linen shirt and then set off for home, a distance of about three miles. He "was jumping over a log, [when] a man sprang up from behind it and gave him a heavy blow with a gun. Joseph turned around and knocked him down, then ran at the top of his speed." The chase continued. "About half a mile farther he was attacked again in the same manner as before; he knocked this man down

in like manner as the former and ran on again; and before he reached home he was assaulted the third time." He entered the Smith home "speechless from fright and the fatigue of running."[9] He had broken his thumb in one of the struggles, but the plates were unharmed.

Joseph had asked Hyrum for the loan of a sturdy chest in which to keep the record. When Hyrum heard that Joseph had the plates at home, he "sprang from the table, caught the chest, turned it upside down, and emptying its contents

on the floor, left the house instantly with the chest on his shoulder" so his brother could use it.[10] Joseph hid the records under the hearth stones in the Smith home. He moved them to his father's cooper shop. He stashed them in a barrel of beans.

Finally, Joseph and Emma took the plates and fled New York. Their friend Martin Harris, a prominent farmer, financed their exit to Emma's family home in Pennsylvania. The Hales welcomed the two; Emma was two months pregnant.

Joseph's father-in-law, Isaac, was not impressed with what he contemptuously called the "wonderful book of plates."[11] He "was allowed to feel the weight of the box,"[12] but that was not enough for the crusty Isaac, who wanted to see the gold plates. He informed Joseph that nothing would be allowed in his house that he could not see, and he pressed the young man to abandon his religious pursuit and settle down to steady farm labor. The growing friction prompted Joseph and Emma to move into a two-room house not far from the Hale family home.

The plates "lay in a box under our bed for months,"[13] said Emma, and "on the [table in our home] without any attempt at concealment, wrapped in a small linen tablecloth, which I had given him to fold them in. I once felt . . . the plates, as they thus lay on the table, tracing their outline and shape. They seemed to be pliable like thick paper, and would rustle with a metallic sound when the edges were moved by the thumb, as one does sometimes thumb the edges of the book."[14]

Emma served as Joseph's scribe as he translated the record those first months. "[He] would dictate to me hour after hour; and when returning after meals, or after interruptions, he would at once begin where he left off, without either seeing the manuscript or having any portion of it read to him," she said years later. "This was a usual thing for him to do. It would have been improbable that a learned man could

ALBANY
FAYETTE
COLESVILLE
HARMONY
New York
Pennsylvania

do this; and, for one so ignorant and unlearned as he was, it was simply impossible."[15]

In the spring of 1828, Martin Harris arrived in Harmony to help. Joseph had copied some of the characters and translated them for Martin to show to Charles Anthon, a highly regarded scholar of classical studies at Columbia College in New York. Initially,  Professor Anthon gave Martin a certificate stating "that they were true characters, and that the translation of such of them as had been translated was also correct." But when he asked how Joseph had found the plates, the response that they were presented by an angel so provoked the scholar that he took back the certificate and "tore it to pieces, saying that there was no such thing now as ministering angels."[16]

Not long after the Anthon incident, Joseph yielded to Martin's pressure to let him show the first 116 pages of the translation to his skeptical wife. Meanwhile, Emma gave birth to their first son, Alvin, who died the same day he was born, June 15, 1828. For two weeks Emma's life hung in the balance, and Joseph cared for her.

When Emma began to rally, Joseph left her in the care of her mother. Desperate to retrieve the translation, he took the stage to Palmyra and walked twenty miles through the woods to the Harris farm. To Joseph's horror, Martin reported that the pages had disappeared.

Joseph agonized that he had "let the writing go out of [his] possession." Said his mother of his reaction, "He wept and groaned, and walked the floor continually."[17] The family grieved, "for it now appeared that all which we had so fondly anticipated, and which had been the source of so much secret gratification, had in a moment fled, and fled forever."[18]

All was not lost, however. Joseph recorded being chastised by God for what had happened: "Repent of that which thou hast done which is contrary to the commandment which I gave you," but he also was encouraged, "thou art still chosen, and art again called to the work."[19]

He began translating again in the fall, but intermittently. In revelation, Joseph was told

WHEN I THINK OF the relationship between Joseph and Emma, I almost think of a grand love story. I think they adored each other. . . . And she had a lot to put up with. She was an energetic, capable, loving, trusting, enthusiastic woman. She had to be, I think, to carry out with the prophet what had to be done. She had to do a lot independently. And once again this, to me, indicates a wonderful relationship that they had, that they could trust each other. He was away from home so much of the time.

—ELAINE L. JACK, FORMER RELIEF SOCIETY GENERAL PRESIDENT, THE CHURCH OF JESUS CHRIST OF LATTER-DAY SAINTS

that evil men had stolen the translation and would try to discredit him by altering the text. He was told not to retranslate the missing text but to turn to other plates in his possession that covered the same period.

BECAUSE OF THE GREAT WORK THAT THE PROPHET MORMON HAD PERFORMED, ABRIDGING AND PREPARING THOSE RECORDS SO THAT HIS SON MORONI COULD ULTIMATELY PLACE THEM IN THE HILL CUMORAH, THE BOOK CARRIES THE NAME OF THE PROPHET MORMON.

—DR. RICHARD BUSHMAN, COLUMBIA UNIVERSITY

The next spring, a young schoolteacher named Oliver Cowdery joined Joseph as his scribe. Oliver had been boarding with the Smiths in New York and had become intrigued by the family's account of Joseph and the plates. Of their work together, Oliver said: "These were days never to be forgotten—to sit under the sound of a voice dictated by the inspiration of heaven, awakened the utmost gratitude of this bosom." Day after day Oliver "continued, uninterrupted, to write from his mouth, as he translated . . . the history, or record, called 'The Book of Mormon.'"[20]

Since Joseph had little time to farm his

makeshift homestead on the Susquehanna River, he and Emma had to make do the best they could. Joseph Knight arrived with supplies at a particularly bleak time. "I bought a Barrel of Mackerel and some lined paper for writing," said Knight, "nine or ten Bushels of grain and five or six Bushels [of] taters and a pound of tea, and I went Down to see him and they ware in want."[21]

In Pennsylvania, as in New York, antagonism soon surfaced. To many, Joseph's efforts were peculiar, even intolerable. The neighbors were uncomfortable with his talk of angels, ancient records, restored teachings, and new scripture. That spring of 1829, tensions began to flare in both Harmony and nearby South Bainbridge. "We had been threatened with being mobbed from time to time,"[22] said Joseph of the mood of the citizenry.

When some of the local Presbyterians converted to the new faith, the town fathers and clergy sought to blunt Joseph's influence by having him tried as a "disorderly person."[23] His attorney, John Reid, who represented Joseph often in the years to come, recounted: "These amazing arrests and prosecutions of the Prophet were among the first of the nearly fifty arraignments to which he was forced to submit. Not once during all these court trials was he proven guilty of any crime, for he was a law-abiding citizen."[24]

Again, Joseph was forced to take the plates to safety. Lodging at the home of Peter and Mary Whitmer, ninety-five miles north in

Fayette, New York, the young prophet finished the last 150 pages of the translation.

For months, translating the records had consumed Joseph's attention. Still, he could not ignore his family responsibilities. "One morning when he was getting ready to continue the translation, something went wrong

nothing save he was humble and faithful."[25]

The plates were now shown for the first time to three men who would act as witnesses. Their testimony was placed at the front of the text of the Book of Mormon:

"Be it known unto all nations, kindreds, tongues, and people, unto whom this work

JOSEPH SMITH WAS *twenty-three years old when he began to translate the Book of Mormon. He had only a superficial education. He dictated the manuscript within a period of about sixty days. There was no research, there was no cross-checking, there was no editing; it was a remarkable accomplishment.*

—ELDER DALLIN H. OAKS, THE CHURCH OF JESUS CHRIST OF LATTER-DAY SAINTS

about the house and [Joseph] was put out about it," described David Whitmer, another associate who later became a witness of the plates. It was "something that Emma . . . had done," according to David. "Oliver and I went upstairs and Joseph came up soon after to continue the translation but he could not do anything. He could not translate a single syllable. He went downstairs, out into the orchard, and made supplication to the Lord; was gone about an hour—came back to the house, and asked Emma's forgiveness and then came upstairs where we were and then the translation went on all right. He could do

shall come: That we . . . have seen the plates. . . . And we also know that they have been translated by the gift and power of God, for his voice hath declared it unto us. . . . And we declare with words of soberness, that an angel of God came down from heaven, and he brought and laid before our eyes, that we beheld and saw the plates, and the engravings thereon; and we know that it is by the grace of God the Father, and our Lord Jesus Christ, that we beheld and bear record that these things are true.

"Oliver Cowdery

"David Whitmer

"Martin Harris"[26]

THE THREE
WITNESSES WERE INTIMATELY INVOLVED IN THE
TRANSLATION OF THE BOOK OF MORMON.

Oliver Cowdery　　　*David Whitmer*　　　*Martin Harris*

MARTIN HARRIS WAS AN EARLY ALLY,

BENEFACTOR, AND CHURCH LEADER. OLIVER

"WROTE WITH [HIS] PEN THE INTIRE

BOOK OF MORMON (SAVE A FEW PAGES) AS IT FELL

FROM THE LIPS OF THE PROPHET" AND

WAS A PROMINENT FIGURE IN ESTABLISHING THE

CHURCH.[27] WHEN PENNSYLVANIA ERUPTED,

IT WAS DAVID WHITMER WHO FERRIED JOSEPH

AND THE PLATES TO SAFE HAVEN.

The Whitmer family, God-fearing Presbyterians, quickly embraced Joseph and his work. As one of the three witnesses to the Book of Mormon, David described that he beheld "a dazzlingly brilliant light that surpassed in brightness even the sun at noonday and . . . a personage clothed in white and near him a table containing the ancient artifacts."[28]

Each of these three men later broke with Joseph Smith and the church he established, but none ever denied his testimony as printed in the Book of Mormon. Oliver and Martin eventually rejoined the church; David never did.

Over a period of fifty years, David was interviewed by dozens of journalists about his intimacy with the Book of Mormon. In 1881 this statement was published in several news-

papers, including the *Richmond Conservator* in Missouri and the *Chicago Times* in Illinois: "I wish now, standing as it were, in the very sunset of life, and in the fear of God, once for all, to make this public statement: That I have never at any time denied that testimony, or any part thereof, which has so long since been published with that Book, as one of the three witnesses. Those who know me best, well know that I have always adhered to that testimony. And that no man may be misled or doubt my present views in regard to the same, I do again affirm the truth of all my statements, as then made and published."

There was a time for me when the knowledge that the three witnesses had left the church was difficult. How could someone who had experienced what they had experienced—to see an angel, to handle sacred records, to hear the voice of God—how could someone of that type leave the church? And yet as the years have gone by, it appears to me that perhaps the most significant thing I've come to know is that although they left the church, they never denied their testimony of what they had experienced, especially their testimony of the truthfulness of the Book of Mormon. If ever they had the opportunity to show the sham of it all, to expose the ludicrousness of Joseph Smith's whole program, that would have been it.

But in a strange way they left the church for petty jealousies, for silly little things, littleness of soul, but [they] did not feel they could deny what they once experienced. Each of them to their dying breath testified that what they'd experienced with Joseph Smith was true and real.

—Dr. Robert Millet,
Brigham Young University

He stated consistently and firmly, "He that hath an ear to hear, let him hear; it was no delusion! What is written is written—and he that readeth let him understand."[29]

At this point, three or four dozen people believed in the divinity of Joseph's calling. "The Lord has now caused the plates to be shown to three more besides myself," said Joseph. "I feel as if I was relieved of a burden which was almost too heavy for me to bear, and it rejoices my soul, that I am not any longer to be entirely alone in the world."[30]

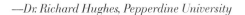

W̲E FIND MANY PEOPLE IN THE UNITED STATES IN THE EARLY NINETEENTH CENTURY LOOKING FOR SOMETHING THAT WENT FAR BEYOND HUMAN REASON. THEY'RE LOOKING FOR DIVINE REASON. THEY'RE LOOKING FOR SPIRITUAL POWER. AND THAT'S EXACTLY WHAT JOSEPH SMITH BROUGHT. . . . JOSEPH SMITH IS A MAN WHO HAS COMMUNED WITH GOD. HE BRINGS POWER FROM ON HIGH IN A WAY THAT OTHER HUMAN BEINGS CAN'T. . . . HE HAD THE WORD FROM GOD. THE WORD FROM ON HIGH. NO ONE ELSE COULD MAKE THAT KIND OF CLAIM.

—*Dr. Richard Hughes, Pepperdine University*

Another eight men—Joseph's father, his brothers Hyrum and Samuel, and Christian, Jacob, Peter, and John Whitmer and their brother-in-law Hiram Page—described being shown the plates by Joseph. Mary Whitmer told of being shown the plates one morning as she was going to milk the cows. She later related that her visitor was an old man who said to her, "You have been very faithful and diligent in your labors, but you are tired because of the increase of your toil, it is proper therefore that you should receive a witness that your faith may be strengthened."[31]

Getting the book published was Joseph's next formidable task. He applied for a copyright in the Northern District of New York on June 11, 1829, and then set about finding a printer. Two firms were approached in nearby Rochester. One scoffed at the proposal to publish the book because of its purported origin; the other quoted an exorbitant price. Joseph and Oliver finally persuaded Egbert B. Grandin, the twenty-three-year-old printer of the local Palmyra newspaper, to accept the commission. Martin Harris, now one of the three witnesses, mortgaged his farm to pay the three-thousand-dollar printing bill.

John H. Gilbert, one of the typesetters in Grandin's shop, described the manuscript as presented "on foolscap paper closely written and legible, but not a punctuation mark from beginning to end." As a precaution Joseph had asked Oliver to recopy the entire manuscript; it was delivered in twenty-four-page sections. The first installment was brought to the shop by Hyrum Smith. According to Gilbert, "He had it under his vest, and vest and coat closely buttoned over it. At night [Hyrum] smith came and got the manuscript, and with the same precaution carried it away." When Gilbert called attention to a grammatical error and asked if he should correct it, "Martin Harris consulted with [Hyrum] Smith a short time, and turned to me and said, 'The Old Testament is ungrammatical, set it as it is written.'"[32] Gilbert did punctuate it "to make it read."[33]

"I told the brethren that the Book of Mormon was the most correct of any book on earth, . . . and a man would get nearer to God by abiding by its precepts, than by any other book."[34]

THE FIVE thousand copies of the Book of Mormon represented a bold undertaking not only for the regional press but for Joseph and his supporters. On March 26, 1830, books were offered for sale for $1.25. There were no buyers. Pomeroy Tucker, editor of the *Wayne Sentinel*, scoffed, "the book . . . fell dead before the public."[35] Locals had pledged in a mass meeting not to purchase the "golden Bible" and to discourage others from securing copies as well.

IT SEEMS to me the Book of Mormon was another element that had enormous appeal to the American people, mainly because it was such an American book. I mean, here's the story of ancient Jews, and they leave Palestine and they sail and they sail and finally dock in the Americas. And it's the story of Jesus Christ coming to America. It's the story of the Gospel to the Americas. So this is another dimension of Smith's enormous appeal. It's a very American tradition and a very American book.

—DR. RICHARD HUGHES, PEPPERDINE UNIVERSITY

The Book of Mormon, nearly six hundred pages in its first printing, was what Joseph called the "keystone" of the new religion and another witness of Jesus Christ. Throughout his ministry Joseph would affirm its divine purpose:

But the believers were undaunted. Avid missionaries soon began distributing the new scripture. Samuel Smith, the prophet's younger brother, was one of the first. He presented a copy to the Young family in upstate New York,

The Book of Mormon
vaulted Joseph to national
attention, and his followers were
soon called "Mormons."

and Brigham Young, who later became the senior apostle of the church and Joseph's successor, read it with interest. Said Brigham,

HAVING THIS BOOK GAVE THEM POWER. HIS FRIENDS WERE AWARE OF THE POWER OF HAVING THE WRITTEN DOCUMENT. THE OTHER GROUPS WHO NEVER PROSPERED NEVER HAD A DOCUMENT. —*Dr. Gordon Wood, Brown University*

"[I] sought to become acquainted with the people who professed to believe it."[36]

W. W. Phelps, editor of New York's *Ontario Phoenix*, said, "By that book I found a key to the holy prophets; and by that book began to unfold the mysteries of God, and I was made glad. Who can . . . estimate the worth of such a book?"[37]

"I arose from its perusal with a strong conviction on my mind, that its pages were graced with the pen of inspiration," said Reverend Orson Spencer, graduate of New York's Union College and the Theological Seminary at Hamilton, New York. "I was surprised that so little fault could be found with a book of such magnitude, treating, as it did, of such diversified subjects, through a period of so many generations. It appeared to me that no enemy to truth

or godliness would ever take the least interest in publishing the contents of such a book."[38]

As historian Grant McMurray observes, "By creating the Book of Mormon, Joseph Smith produced the notion of an open canon of scripture that said in effect, the last word has not been heard from God. There's more to know and God will reveal that in God's own time. That's a pretty radical message. It's a revolutionary message."[39]

The book had its detractors. Some viewed it as a hoax, an affront to orthodox Christianity. Though the churches in Joseph's hometown disagreed on a host of doctrines and disciplines, they agreed on one thing: the blasphemous nature of Joseph and his book. The *Palmyra Freeman* suggested that the book was "the greatest piece of superstition that has come within our knowledge."[40] Said the *Palmyra Reflector*, "The age of miracles has again arrived, and if the least reliance can be placed upon the assertions daily made by the 'Gold Bible' apostles (which is somewhat doubtful), no prophet, since the destruction of Jerusalem by Titus, has performed half so many wonders as have been attributed to that spindle-shanked ignoramus: Joe Smith. This fellow appears to possess the quintessence of impudence, while his fellow laborers are not far behind in a greater or lesser degree."[41]

The *Rochester Daily Advertiser* commented, "A viler imposition was never practiced. It is an evidence of fraud, blasphemy, and credulity, shocking both to Christians and Moralists."[42]

Alexander Campbell, whose own religious movement was garnering attention and converts, announced his view of the new scripture: "I would as soon compare a bat to the American eagle, a mouse to a mammoth . . . as to contrast it with a single chapter in all the writings of the Jewish or Christian prophets."[43] Other papers as far east as Boston labeled the work "fanatacism" and "blasphemy."[44]

The Book of Mormon vaulted Joseph to national attention, and his followers were soon called "Mormons." James Gordon Bennett of the *New York Morning Courier and Enquirer* stated, "You have heard of MORMONISM— who has not? Paragraph has followed paragraph in the newspaper, recounting the movements, detailing their opinions and surprising distant readers with the traits of a singularly new religious sect."[45]

"It was extremely upsetting to the people locally," says Dr. Mario DePillis of Amherst College, "because they saw this young man claiming to discover a new scripture, the socalled Golden Bible, that was reported in the newspapers. And it was well known. When he began to make converts, that was extremely upsetting to the local ministers and to the religious leaders in the country at large.

"As I see it, the reason is that they almost immediately saw that Joseph Smith was constructing, so to speak, an entirely new wing onto the Judeo-Christian edifice. He claimed to be Christian, yes, he claimed devotion to Jesus Christ as God, but redefined some of the basic beliefs in such a manner that it was an entirely new religious tradition."[46]

But Joseph spoke with confidence, "Great opposition and much persecution followed the believers of its authenticity; but it had now come to pass that truth had sprung out of the earth; and righteousness had looked down from heaven—so we feared not our opponents, knowing that we had both truth and righteousness on our side; that we had both the Father and the Son, because we had the doctrines of Christ, and abided in them."[47]

I N MY WORK, I have talked very much about how the Book of Mormon legitimates Joseph Smith. The Book of Mormon says that when the book comes forth, a prophet will come forth—and his name, like that of his father, will be Joseph. Those are the kinds of signals that this is the right person; this is really a prophet. So if you take the Book of Mormon for what it claims to be, it legitimates Joseph Smith. And then Joseph Smith at the head of the church legitimates the church as a true church. —Dr. Jan Shipps, Indiana University

4

LESS THAN TWO weeks after
the Book of Mormon went on sale in
Palmyra, Joseph Smith formally
established a church. On Tuesday,
April 6, 1830, about sixty men and
women attended the organizing
meeting in Fayette, New York, and
accepted the twenty-four-year-old
Joseph as "a seer, a translator, a
prophet, an apostle of Jesus Christ."[1]

OSEPH viewed his labor as restoring the gospel of Jesus Christ and the primitive church. He instructed the people "to build up the Church" and exhorted them "to be faithful in all things for this is the work of God."[2]

In the years ahead, Joseph would give shape to the new religion as he pronounced doctrine, identified the official name as The Church of Jesus Christ of Latter-day Saints, defined a structure of church offices, put the priesthood of God to work, announced temples and sacred ordinances, and introduced the concept of a Zion people. This humble beginning, he told the people, was "destined to bring about the destruction of the powers of darkness, the renovation of the earth, the glory of God, and the salvation of the human family."[3]

The previous spring, while translating the Book of Mormon, Joseph had been puzzled by references to what he later called "the holy order of God."[4] Passages like "none received

authority to preach or to teach except it were . . . from God"[5] prompted the question of who had the authority to baptize. Joseph and Oliver stopped translating and prayed for an answer.

They later recounted that an angel, John the Baptist, appeared and conferred upon them "the Priesthood of Aaron."[6] They said that having that authority qualified them to baptize each other "by immersion for the remission of sins." There, in the Susquehanna River in northeastern Pennsylvania, Joseph baptized Oliver; Oliver then baptized Joseph.

"Immediately on our coming up out of the water after we had been baptized, we experienced great and glorious blessings from our Heavenly Father," said Joseph. "I prophesied concerning the rise of this church, and many other things connected with the Church, and this generation of the children of men."[7]

Oliver later wrote, "While the world were racked and distracted—while millions were groping as the blind for the wall, and while

Joseph Smith didn't set out to reform any of the established churches. This occurred during the earlier years, coming out of the dark ages. The Renaissance and numerous churches arose in the world as reformed churches for the most part, trying to bring about a reformation from the abuses which they saw in the church from which they sprang. Joseph Smith on the other hand was a restorationist, in contrast with a reformist. He restored that which was on the earth anciently—the teachings, the doctrines, the practices of the Savior. —PRESIDENT GORDON B. HINCKLEY, THE CHURCH OF JESUS CHRIST OF LATTER-DAY SAINTS

On May 15, 1829, "While we were thus employed, praying and calling upon the Lord," Joseph wrote of his and Oliver's experience at the Susquehanna River, "a messenger from heaven descended in a cloud of light."[8]

In the Susquehanna River in
northeastern Pennsylvania, Joseph baptized Oliver;
Oliver then baptized Joseph.

all men were resting upon uncertainty, . . . our eyes beheld—our ears heard. . . . Where was room for doubt? Nowhere."[9]

Not long after this, they described receiving the Melchizedek Priesthood from the ancient Apostles Peter, James, and John. This additional priesthood gave them the power to bestow the Holy Ghost. Thus the groundwork was laid for the authoritative organization of the new church.

At that first meeting of the church, several

ther people could point to scripture. Or they could point to their interpretation of scripture. Or they could point to their particular creeds or confessions of faith. Joseph said, I spoke with God. God spoke with me in the woods. That's power and authority, and it spoke to a lot of Americans very powerfully in the early nineteenth century.

—DR. RICHARD HUGHES, PEPPERDINE UNIVERSITY

in attendance asked to be baptized, including Joseph's parents. Following the baptisms, Joseph exclaimed, "Praise to my God! that I lived to see my own father baptized into the true Church of Jesus Christ."[10] Other members described with reverence the experience of having hands laid upon their heads to confer the Holy Ghost. "The Holy Ghost was poured out upon us to a

very great degree," expressed Joseph. "We all praised the Lord, and rejoiced exceedingly."[11]

Residents of Colesville, New York, formed the backbone of the church in its early days, but it spread quickly. Soon missionaries headed east to New England, north to Canada, and west to the far frontier, their satchels filled with copies of the Book of Mormon. "Thousands

> **"OUR EYES BEHELD—OUR EARS HEARD. WHERE WAS ROOM FOR DOUBT? NOWHERE."**

flocked about us daily," said Parley P. Pratt, an early convert who accepted the assignment to proselyte for the new church, "some to be taught, some for curiosity, some to obey the gospel, and some to dispute it or resist it."[12]

Initially missionaries returned to the communities of their youth, hoping to interest their families and friends in the new faith. Some, like the prophet's uncle John Smith, were converted. Others rejected the message, as Orson Hyde reported, "We took our things and left them, and tears from all eyes freely ran . . . but it was like piercing my heart; and all I can say is 'The Will of the Lord Be Done.'"[13]

A few missionaries were directed west to

preach to the Indians. Stopping in Kirtland, Ohio, they found the residents particularly receptive to their message. Sidney Rigdon, a prominent local minister, "got so engaged in reading the Book of Mormon," his son related, "that it was hard for him to quit long enough to eat his meals."[14] Sidney was converted, along with most of his congregation, and later became a counselor to Joseph and one of his most trusted friends.

The *Painesville Telegraph*, published just nine miles from Kirtland, noted on November 16, 1830, that twenty to thirty people had been baptized into the new faith. Two weeks

in possession of as much light and knowledge as had flowed into my mind from that source. . . . I counted the cost, to myself and family, of embracing such views, until I could read it like the child his alphabet, either upward or downward. The expense I viewed through unavoidable tears, both in public and private, by night and by day; I said, however, the Lord He is God, I can, I will embrace the truth."[16]

The new church gave rise to antagonism. To perform baptisms, Joseph and others "erected a dam across a stream of water," but during the night a mob collected and tore it down. Joseph

THE RELIGIOUS IMPULSE—THE RELIGIOUS FERMENT, IF YOU WILL—IS QUITE UNIQUE AT THIS PERIOD. THERE IS EMERGING A WHOLE NEW ATTITUDE TOWARD RELIGION, A WHOLE NEW ATTITUDE OF THE KIND OF MINISTERS THESE PEOPLE WANTED. UNLIKE THEIR COLONIAL FOREBEARERS, WHO WERE LOOKING FOR MEN WHO WERE WELL EDUCATED AT PLACES LIKE YALE AND HARVARD AND PRINCETON AND SUCH, THEY WERE LOOKING FOR MEN WHO COULD SPEAK FROM THE SPIRIT OF THEIR OWN INVOLVEMENT WITH THE DIVINE AND TELL WHAT THAT WAS LIKE. **—DR. GORDON WOOD, BROWN UNIVERSITY**

later, the paper reported a "rising of one hundred . . . who have embraced the ideas and assertions of Joseph Smith, Jr., many of them respectable for intelligency and piety."[15]

Reverend Orson Spencer, who had been drawn to the spirited young Smith and his new religion, agonized over his decision: "I cursed Mormonism in my heart, and regretted being

claimed that the "mob had been instigated to this act of molestation by certain sectarian priests of the neighborhood, who began to consider their craft in danger, and took this plan to stop the progress of the truth."[17] Back in Harmony, Joseph's enemies advertised a $5 reward for any sightings of the prophet in the community.[18]

Reverend Diedrich Willer charged: "The

greatest imposter of our times in the field of religion is no doubt a certain Joseph Smith. This new sect should not cause the Christian Church great astonishment. The past centuries have also had religious off-shoots. They have all been absorbed in the Sea of the Past and marked with the stamp of oblivion. This will also be the lot of the

A STEADY STREAM OF CHURCH MEMBERS FLOWED TO OHIO.

Mormonites, and, I hope, while it is still in the bud."[19]

In December 1830, Joseph made a bold move that further defined the church and its people. He announced that he had received a revelation that commanded the faithful—as the latter-day hosts of Israel—to gather in Kirtland. "Gathering" the members would become a distinctive feature of Joseph's teachings. Over the next fifteen years, thousands would leave their professions, their homes, and even their families to come together in the fold. "As might be expected, we were obliged to make great sacrifices of our property,"[20] said Newel Knight of his move to relocate as instructed. Joseph promised that by "a concentration of action, and a unity of effort, we can only accomplish the great work of the last days which we could not do in our

remote and scattered condition."[21] He and Emma arrived in Kirtland in February 1831.

Within months, a steady stream of church members flowed to Ohio from Fayette, Colesville, and Manchester, New York. "They came . . . in every conceivable manner, some with horses, oxen, and vehicles rough and rude, while others had walked all or part of the distance," wrote the *Geauga County Recorder*, into whose community the new members came. "The future 'City of the Saints' appeared like one besieged. Every available house, shop, hut, or barn was filled to its utmost capacity. Even boxes were roughly extemporized and used for shelter until something more permanent could be secured."[22]

"When wagon loads of grown people and children came in from the country to meeting, Joseph would make his way to as many of the wagons as he well could and cordially shake the hand of each person," recalled Louisa Y. Littlefield. "Every child and young babe in the company were especially noticed by him and tenderly taken by the hand, with his kind words and blessings."[23]

"He didn't appear exactly as I expected to see a Prophet of God," said Jonathan Crosby, a cabinetmaker who had converted and moved to Kirtland in 1835. "However I was not stumbled at all. I found him to be a friendly, cheerful,

*G*ATHERED COMMUNITY IS, I THINK, ONE OF JOSEPH SMITH'S

BEST IDEAS, BUT IT'S NOT INTUITIVELY OBVIOUS WHY,

PARTICULARLY GIVEN THE AMERICAN LANDSCAPE. IT IS A RISK,

THE NOTION OF BRINGING PEOPLE TOGETHER WITHIN

A FIXED BOUNDARY TO INVENT A SENSE OF TOGETHERNESS, TO

INSIST ON PEOPLE COMING TO THIS COMMUNITY, COMING TO

KIRTLAND, COMING TO MISSOURI, COMING TO NAUVOO,

OR EVEN MORE HEROIC, MAKING THAT LONG TREK OUT ACROSS TO

THE GREAT SALT LAKE BASIN. IT'S JUST AMAZING.

I MEAN, THERE'S NO NARRATIVE IN RELIGIOUS HISTORY THAT EVEN

COMES CLOSE. BUT IT WORKED. AND IT WORKED IN

SURPRISING WAYS. —*Dr. Larry Moore, Cornell University*

pleasant, agreeable man. I could not help liking him."[24] One of Joseph's closest friends, Benjamin F. Johnson, said, "I was closely associated with the Prophet Joseph Smith, was his trusted friend and business partner, his relative, and bosom friend. And I knew him as the purest, the truest and noblest of manly men."[25]

J OSEPH SMITH TAUGHT AS EFFECTIVELY AS ANYTHING THAT MEN AND WOMEN HAVE THE CAPACITY TO GROW AND DEVELOP AND ASPIRE TO SPIRITUAL GREATNESS. NOT JUST PROPHETS, NOT JUST APOSTLES, NOT JUST OFFICE HOLDERS, BUT THAT ALL MEN AND WOMEN HAVE THE OPPORTUNITY TO BECOME GODLIKE. AND SO JOSEPH SMITH'S EFFORT WAS TO TAKE THE MEN AND WOMEN AND BRING THEM WITH HIM. THE FACT THAT MOST OF HIS LIFE, ESPECIALLY HIS MATURE LIFE, THEY CALLED HIM BROTHER JOSEPH, THAT'S NOT INCONSEQUENTIAL. IT IMPLIES A RESPECT. BUT IT IMPLIES A CLOSENESS THAT THEY FELT TO HIM.

—DR. ROBERT MILLET, BRIGHAM YOUNG UNIVERSITY

Crowded around Joseph were not only the faithful but the curious. Fifty-three-year-old

John Johnson and his wife, Alice (or Elsa), ventured from their home in Hiram, a community south of Kirtland, to see the man many were calling a prophet of God. As the group engaged Joseph in a discussion about supernatural gifts, someone asked, pointing to Mrs. Johnson and her lame arm, "Has God given any power to man now on the earth to cure her?" The conversation soon shifted to another theme, but the question had caught Joseph's attention. He grasped Alice's hand and, in a "solemn and impressive manner," said, "Woman, in the name of the Lord Jesus Christ I command thee to be whole." The group watched, stunned, as Alice Johnson lifted her arm in the air. From that moment on she was able to see to her household work "without difficulty or pain."[26]

Not surprisingly, the Johnsons opened their home to Joseph and his family. While living there, Joseph worked on revising portions of the Bible, believing that "many important points touching the salvation of man, had been taken

The Bible was a powerful book, but revelation trumps the Bible. Joseph felt that he had the authority to actually change the words of the Bible by force of his own revelation. He added long passages coming through revelation, too. So for Mormons in his time, and today, the revelation is what they heed above all.

—DR. RICHARD BUSHMAN, COLUMBIA UNIVERSITY

from the Bible, or lost before it was compiled."[27] Problems in the text were a result, he said, of translation errors, loss of original text, and some deliberate recrafting in earlier times.

While Joseph was translating St. John's

Gospel with the help of Sidney Rigdon, he declared: "The Lord touched the eyes of our understanding and they were opened, and the glory of the Lord shone round about. And we beheld the glory of the Son, on the right hand of the Father, and received his fulness; And saw the holy angels, and them who are sanctified before his throne, worshiping God, and the Lamb." He continued his account of the vision: "This is the testimony, last of all which we give of him: That he lives! For we saw him, even on the right hand of God; and we heard the voice bearing record that he is the Only Begotten of the Father."[28]

A handful of close associates were present at the time. Philo Dibble reported: "Joseph would at intervals say, 'What do I see?' as one might say while looking out the window and beholding what all in the room could not see. Then he would relate what he had seen or what he was looking at. Then Sidney replied, 'I see the same.' Presently Sidney would say, 'What do I see?' and would repeat what he had seen or was seeing, and Joseph would reply, 'I see the same.'

"This manner of conversation was repeated at short intervals to the end of the vision . . . which . . . was over an hour. . . . Joseph sat firmly and calmly all the time in the midst of a magnificent glory, but Sidney sat limp and pale, apparently as limber as a rag, observing which, Joseph remarked, smilingly, 'Sidney is not used to it as I am.'"[29]

Joseph claimed to open the heavens not only as a translator but also as a revelator. Sixty-five revelations were received in Ohio from February of 1831 to July of 1837. Many offered counsel and comfort to church members. Others directed the affairs of the church, including the organization

THIS IS THE KEY TO UNDERSTANDING JOSEPH SMITH AND TO UNDER-STANDING MORMONISM, I AM CONVINCED: IT IS THE LITERALNESS, THE EXPERIENCING THE SAME THINGS THAT ARE DESCRIBED IN THE SCRIPTURES. MORMONISM TAKES THE SCRIPTURES AND BRINGS THEM INTO LIFE—LITERALLY RECAPITULATES THE SCRIPTURES. NOW, IF YOU GET THAT UNDERSTANDING OF JOSEPH SMITH'S UNDERSTANDING OF WHAT WAS GOING ON, THEN YOU BEGIN TO SEE THAT THIS COULD NOT HAVE BEEN JUST SOMEBODY MAKING IT UP AS HE WENT ALONG. —DR. JAN SHIPPS, INDIANA UNIVERSITY

of units called "stakes" in 1834 and the setting in place of the Quorum of the Twelve Apostles and the Council of the Seventy in 1835.

Parley P. Pratt described the method of recording these revelations: "Each sentence was uttered slowly and very distinctly, and with a pause between each, sufficiently long for it to be recorded, by an ordinary writer in long hand. This was the manner in which all his written revelations were dictated and written. . . . As he dictated them so they stood."[30]

One of Joseph's followers, William E. McLellin, challenged Joseph's role, suggesting that he too could compose revelations. "As the wisest man, in his own estimation, having more learning than sense, [he] endeavored to write a commandment like unto one of the least of the Lord's, but failed," Joseph said. "It was an awful responsibility to write in the name of the Lord."[31]

In 1833, Joseph instituted the School of the Prophets to prepare missionaries to teach the gospel and to elevate the minds of the people. The school's curriculum included courses in history, political science, languages, literature, and theology. In 1836, Joseph hired Dr. Joshua Seixas for $320 to teach a seven-week course of Hebrew to his cadre of farmers, merchants, and tradesmen. Joseph counseled his wife, Emma, by revelation, "Thy time shall be given to writing, and to learning much."[32] While in Kirtland, she made ninety selections for the first hymnal of the Church.

The school met initially in convert Newel K. Whitney's store. Bothered by studying spiritual matters in a cloud of smoke, and prompted by Emma, who had to clean a floor splattered with tobacco juice, Joseph asked God for guidance. He then communicated to his followers the Word of Wisdom, a health code forbidding the use of tobacco, wine, strong drink, and "hot drinks," which were understood to be coffee and tea; it also stressed eating of vegetables, fruits, and grains.

Joseph spoke of receiving revelation for the care of the poor and needy in "the very same order of things as observed by the holy Apostles of old."[33] As converts poured into the area, many with little substance to sustain them, he instituted a system of consecration—a sharing of resources among the members—to help care for them.

JOSEPH'S revelations often included prophecies. Though somewhat isolated from society, he and his followers were politically aware of issues facing the nation. On Christmas Day, 1832, in the midst of a growing rift between President Andrew Jackson and South Carolina, Joseph predicted that the nation would eventually splinter in a bloody conflict: "Verily, thus saith the Lord concerning the wars that will shortly come to pass, beginning at the rebellion of South Carolina, which will eventually terminate in the death and misery of many souls . . . the Southern States shall be divided against the Northern States, and the Southern States will call on other nations, even the nation of Great Britain . . . slaves shall rise up against their masters, who shall be marshaled and disciplined for war."[34]

Thirty years later, the Civil War tore the country in half.

The School of the Prophets first met in an upper room of Newel K. Whitney's store (below). Hyrum's Hebrew Bible (right) illustrates their study of languages.

In 1830, Emma Smith was asked to make a collection of sacred hymns for the church. She selected ninety of those pieces for the first hymnal (left) while in Kirtland.

Zion was to serve as the center of what Joseph called the kingdom of God on earth. Here the people would gather to prepare for the second coming of the Savior and His millennial reign. Kirtland would be maintained as church headquarters, but the growing numbers of arriving saints would be sent on to Missouri to build Zion. For the next seven years, Joseph and other Church leaders would shuttle the nearly nine hundred miles between the two settlements to direct the efforts of the Ohio and Missouri communities.

In June 1831, in company with a handful of others, Joseph set off by wagon, canal boat, stage, and steamer, walking the final 250 miles of unsettled prairie to Independence, Missouri. The Colesville saints followed behind. Emily M. Austin recalled, "People all along the road stared at us as they would at a circus or a caravan. . . . We most truly were a band of pilgrims, started out to seek a better country. . . . We were told [by teamsters] we were the most peaceable and quiet emigrants they had ever carried west; no profanity, no bad language, no gambling, and no drinking."[43]

"On the second day of August," Newel K. Whitney later recorded, "Brother Joseph Smith, Junior, the prophet of God, assisted the Colesville branch to lay the first log as a foundation for Zion in Kaw township, twelve miles west of Independence" in Jackson County, Missouri. For Whitney and the others, "This was truly a season of joy and rejoicing to all the Saints."[44]

The Missouri countryside was lush and green, with rolling hills and rivers. Land was inexpensive, $1.25 an acre. Independence at the time was little more than a rough outpost for explorers, trappers, and traders. For these New York transplants, it was a foreign land. Newel K. Whitney described the challenges

they faced: "We were not accustomed to a frontier life, so things around us seemed new and strange and the work we had to do was of a different nature to that which had been done in the East. Yet we took hold with cheerful hearts, and a determination to do our best, and with all diligence went to work to secure food and prepare for the coming winter."[45]

But the Mormons did not mix well in the

fiercely independent culture of Missouri. Political forces divided on the issue of slavery; Mormons were considered Yankees and hence held suspect by those with southern leanings. In addition, the Mormons believed that the land had been given to them by God and that they

"Little more than two years ago, some two or three of these people made their appearance on the Upper Missouri and they now number some 1,200 souls in this country, and each successive autumn and spring pours forth its swarm among us, with a gradual falling off in

THAT'S THE PART of Mormonism that I like: that event was required. You did not simply believe in your heart and wait for the Lord to save you. But you sold your goods, you got in a wagon with your family, and you went to the place where the holy city was to be erected and there made a life in a new society. . . . I think what galvanized belief was this set of ideas about the coming of the Savior combined with the action people had to take to move their families to the new city, create a Zion society, and build a temple. —*Dr. Richard Bushman, Columbia University*

were to preach salvation to the perverse generation—their neighbors. Their conviction was scorned, as was their communal effort. On the farthest frontier, Joseph and his people were not only peculiar, they embodied a threat to the existing economic, social, and political forces.

The old settlers of Independence saw the Mormons as "deluded fanatics"[46] from the lowest levels of society. Their feelings were clear:

the character of those who compose it; until it seems that those communities from which they have come, were flooding us with the very dregs of their composition."[47]

By 1833 discord hit a fever pitch.

In a plea for guidance and a cry for help, William Phelps wrote to the church leaders in Kirtland, "Brethren, if the Lord will, I should like to know what the honest in heart shall do?

Our clothes are worn out; we want the necessaries of life . . . I am sensible that we shall not be able to live again in Zion, till God or the President rules out the mob. . . . The mob swear if we come we shall die!"[48]

Mobs destroyed the Mormon printing press, tarred and feathered a Mormon leader, and burned Mormon homes. The saints were forced

to flee in the bitter winter weather to Clay County, where they found some refuge in abandoned cabins, crude huts, and tents.

"When we learn your sufferings," wrote Joseph to the Missouri saints, "it awakens every sympathy in our hearts; it weighs us down; we cannot refrain from tears, yet, we are not able to realize, only in part, your sufferings."[49]

Clay County offered temporary asylum, but a longer-term solution was reached in 1835 when Caldwell County was designated by government officials as the Mormon colony, and the refugees moved to this least inhabited part of the state.

In a letter to Emma written on a return trip to Kirtland from Missouri, Joseph wrote of his own soul searching: "I have visited a grove

which is just back of the town almost every day where I can be Secluded from the eyes of any mortal and there give vent to all the feelings of my heart in mediation and praiyr. I have Called to mind all the past moments of my life and am left to morn and Shed tears of Sorrow for my folly in sufering the adversary of my Soul to have so much power over me as he has had in times past but God is merciful and has forgiven my Sins and I rejoice that he Sendeth forth the Comforter unto as many as believe and humbleth themselves before him. . . . I will try to be contented with my lot knowing that God is my friend

I *would not paint Joseph Smith in pastel colors. He was a radical preacher of extreme ideas, very powerful ideas, which had tremendous appeal particularly for those who were on the margins of society. But they were extreme ideas. And he called people to extreme ways of living, dependent upon his authority because he believed that God was speaking in new and profoundly different ways.*
—Dr. Nathan Hatch, University of Notre Dame

in him I shall find comfort I have given my life into his hands I am prepared to go at his Call."[50]

"As my life consisted of activity and unyielding exertions," he declared on another occasion, "I made this one rule: When the Lord commands, do it."[51] This, despite their difficulties, he and his people continued to do.

A HOUSE OF GOD

5

To FORTIFY ZION, JOSEPH ANNOUNCED in 1831 the building of a temple in Kirtland. The Lord had revealed, he later said, that this holy structure was to follow the pattern of biblical times as "a house of prayer, a house of fasting, a house of faith, a house of learning, a house of glory, a house of order, a house of God."[1]

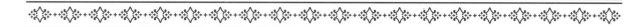

BRIGHAM YOUNG said of the decree, "Without revelation, Joseph could not know what was wanted, any more than any other man, and, without commandment, the Church were too few in number, too weak in faith, and too poor in purse, to attempt such a mighty enterprise."[2] At the time, the members of the church in Kirtland numbered a few hundred; the majority of new converts had been told to gather in Jackson County, Missouri.

Some imagined that a substantial log meetinghouse would serve the purpose, but Joseph made it clear that the temple was to be a structure far more grand. According to Orson Pratt, the details of architecture were "far beyond the experience or training of the members and according to the heavenly pattern that He by His voice had inspired his servants."[3]

Construction of this first latter-day temple, which began in earnest June 5, 1833, would make it possible for the saints to be "endowed with power from on high."[4] Joseph's brother Hyrum initiated the work, striking "the first blow upon the house."[5] He and two others, Reynolds Cahoon and Jared Carter, supervised the construction of the sacred edifice, which resembled a New England meetinghouse. It would cost between forty and sixty thousand dollars, a monumental sum for a people who were sharing their food just to stay alive. Nothing was spared to fashion what the people believed was a house of the Lord. Lucy Mack Smith described their commitment, "There was but one mainspring to all our thoughts and actions, and that was, the building of the Lord's house."[6]

When Joseph outlined what was needed in terms of skill and artistry, Heber C. Kimball said he knew someone who could do the job, but the man, Artemus Millet, lived in Canada and was not a member of the church. Joseph dispatched Brigham Young to convert Millet and bring him to Kirtland for the work. He added that Millet should also bring with him one thousand dollars to assist with the project. Weeks later, Brigham, Artemus, and the money arrived in Kirtland.[7]

Many new members were asked to give more than their time and teams; substantial cash contributions from converts kept the project moving. New Yorker John Tanner loaned Joseph money to purchase the temple site and to provide supplies for the bishop's storehouse. Once a wealthy farmer, he sold his twenty

The temple would cost between forty and sixty thousand dollars, a monumental sum for a people who were sharing their food just to stay alive.

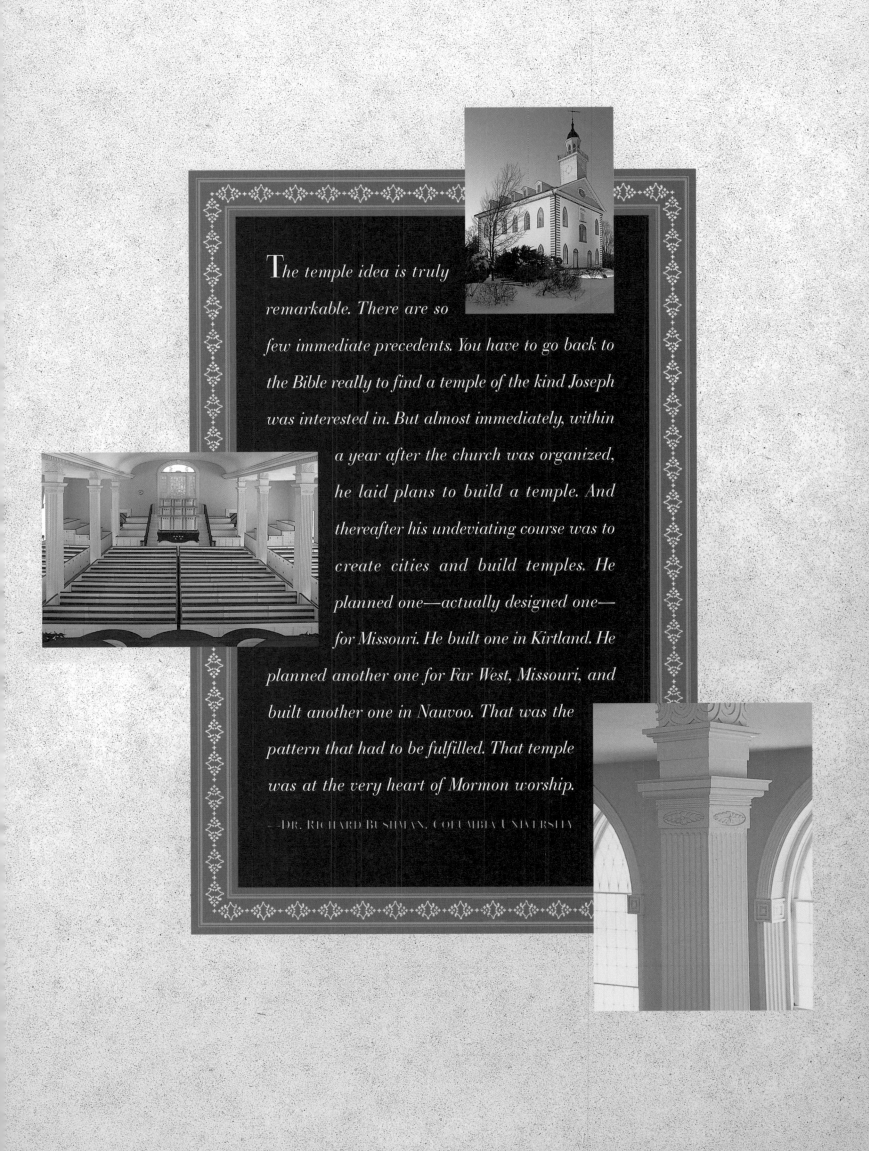

The temple idea is truly remarkable. There are so few immediate precedents. You have to go back to the Bible really to find a temple of the kind Joseph was interested in. But almost immediately, within a year after the church was organized, he laid plans to build a temple. And thereafter his undeviating course was to create cities and build temples. He planned one—actually designed one— for Missouri. He built one in Kirtland. He planned another one for Far West, Missouri, and built another one in Nauvoo. That was the pattern that had to be fulfilled. That temple was at the very heart of Mormon worship.

—DR. RICHARD BUSHMAN, COLUMBIA UNIVERSITY

acres of land, a sawmill, and a gristmill to supply the church with the much-needed funds.[8]

For three years, men donated one day a week to labor on the temple. Some worked on the building full time, receiving meager food supplies and clothing as compensation. Joseph Smith did not exempt himself from the physical labor. "Come brethren," he was known to say, "let us go into the stone quarry and work for the Lord."[9] And work it was. Every available team was used each Saturday to ferry the cut sandstone to the temple site. Oak for the

resurrection; and the sisters now are the first to work on the inside of the temple."[11]

The temple's interior reflected both Federal and Greek Revival style patterns. Elaborate tiered pulpits rose from each end of the main-floor meeting room. Pews blocked the floor into sections, and a grand "window beautiful," adorned by flowering vines meeting at the arch, drew attention to the height and majesty of the room. The upstairs rooms—classrooms and offices—were more simple in design. Wrap-around staircases connected the floors.

> "THE SISTERS ARE ALWAYS FIRST AND FOREMOST IN ALL GOOD WORKS.
> MARY WAS FIRST AT THE RESURRECTION; AND THE SISTERS
> NOW ARE THE FIRST TO WORK ON THE INSIDE OF THE TEMPLE."

beams was cut from nearby forests; only glass and special tools were purchased.

The women likewise organized their efforts: they sewed stockings, pantaloons, and jackets and prepared meals for the laborers. "Our wives were all the time knitting, spinning and sewing," recalled Heber C. Kimball, "and, in fact, I may say doing all kinds of work; they were just as busy as any of us . . . and God will bless them for evermore."[10]

A group of sisters were at work on furnishings inside the temple one day when Joseph stopped by. "You are always on hand," he said. "The sisters are always first and foremost in all good works. Mary was first at the

Construction was a broad communal effort, but not everyone joined in or supported the enterprise. During the winter of 1836, as the saints labored to complete the temple, opposition escalated. Pockets of dissenters with individual frustrations united in a common cause: to stop Joseph. Some did not share the prophet's fervor for religion or his interest in building a community of saints. Their antagonism, which had been voiced early in his ministry, did not subside. Others disapproved of his gathering so many people to Kirtland, straining the resources of the whole community, not just the Mormons. Most troublesome

to Joseph were the increasing numbers of former followers who grew disenchanted with the way he was unfolding the doctrines and practices of the new faith. They became Joseph's most bitter rivals.

Ezra Booth, a former Methodist preacher who converted to Mormonism but quickly became disillusioned, made it his cause to discredit Joseph Smith. In a letter printed in the *Painesville Telegraph* in late 1831, he questioned Joseph's "prudence and stability."[12] Simonds Ryder and Philastus Hurlbut also wrote and lectured against their former leader.

Other religious leaders who were barely able to sustain a congregation on the frontier saw Joseph as taking converts from their small flocks. One Presbyterian minister in Kirtland, Truman Coe, charged, "It is difficult to foretell how long it will take this gust of Fanaticism to spend itself, and die away, and sink to the oblivion of the 100 other which have gone before it. . . . The vice of Mormonism must be accounted one of the most palpable and wide-spread delusions which this country has ever seen; and nothing can equal the zeal of their leaders in its propagation."[13]

Some simply counted the costs of Mormonism as too high. A local minister charged, "If the prophet demand their money for the Lord's treasury, he can have it by uttering a Thus saith the Lord."[14] Joseph's teachings wedded theology and economic phi-losophy, which stretched the religiosity of many. In the temple-building years, two to three hundred left the fold.

Heber C. Kimball said of the tension between the "laborers on the walls" and the discontented in the community during the temple construction, "We had to guard night after night, and . . . were obliged to lie with our fire-locks in our arms, to preserve Brother Joseph's life."[15] On one occasion, Joseph met Wilford Woodruff and stood back studying him before explaining, "Brother Woodruff, I am glad to see you. I hardly know when I meet those who have been my brethren in the Lord, who of them are my friends. They have become so scarce."[16] Brigham Young noted that workers "were holding the sword in one hand to protect themselves from the mob, while they placed the stone and moved the trowel with the other."[17]

Despite these impediments, the structure was finally completed, and a congregation of nearly a thousand packed the first meeting to dedicate the Kirtland Temple. That week of March 27, 1836, the faithful spoke of angels and glorious visions, heralding their experience in a 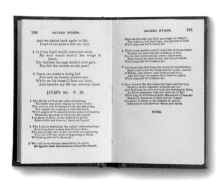 hymn by W. W. Phelps: "We'll sing and we'll shout with the armies of heaven."[18]

Joseph told the saints that the Lord would appear and accept His house and the sacrifice

GOD WAS THERE, HIS ANGELS WERE THERE, THE HOLY GHOST WAS IN THE MIDST OF THE PEOPLE, THE VISIONS OF THE ALMIGHTY WERE OPENED TO THE MINDS OF THE SERVANTS OF THE LIVING GOD. —*Orson Pratt*

of the people. He later described: "The temple was filled with angels, which fact I declared to the congregation. The people of the neighborhood came running together (hearing an unusual sound within, and seeing a bright light like a pillar of fire resting upon the Temple), and were astonished at what was taking place."[19]

"God was there, his angels were there, the Holy Ghost was in the midst of the people, the visions of the Almighty were opened to the minds of the servants of the living God,"[20] testified Orson Pratt of the event. Eliza R. Snow described her experience, "The ceremonies of that dedication may be rehearsed, but no mortal language can describe the heavenly manifestations of that memorable day. Angels appeared to some, while a sense of divine presence was realized by all present."[21] Many compared the spiritual outpourings to the New Testament day of Pentecost.

Descriptions of spiritual appearances were plentiful as the saints participated in services in the temple. "Never until then had I heard a man address his Maker as though He was present listening. There was no ostentation, no raising of the voice as by enthusiasm, but a plain conversational tone," said Daniel Tyler of a prayer offered by Joseph in the temple. "It appeared to me as though . . . I could see the Lord standing facing His humblest of all servants I had ever seen. . . . Whether this was really the case I cannot say; but one thing I can say, it was the

crowning . . . of all the prayers I ever heard."[22]

Those outside the temple also described manifestations. Presendia Huntington said, "A little girl came to my door and in wonder called me out, exclaiming, 'The meeting is on the top of the meeting house!' I went to the door, and there I saw on the temple angels clothed in white covering the roof from end to end. They seemed to be walking to and fro; they appeared and disappeared. The third time they appeared and disappeared before I realized that they were not mortal men. . . . This was in broad daylight in the afternoon."[23]

The week following the dedication, on Easter Sunday, April 3, 1836, Joseph and Oliver described receiving keys of the priesthood as they knelt in prayer. John Taylor observed, "Jesus appeared there, and Moses appeared there, and Moses conferred upon Joseph the keys of the gathering of Israel from the four quarters of the earth, and also the ten tribes."[24]

Joseph wrote of the visitation, "The veil was taken from our minds, and the eyes of our understanding were opened. We saw the Lord standing upon the breast work of the pulpit, before us; and under his feet was a paved work of pure gold, in color like amber. His eyes were as a flame of fire; the hair of his head was white like the pure snow; his countenance shone above the brightness of the sun; and his voice was as the sound of the rushing of great waters, even the voice of Jehovah."[25] That singular moment was a fulfillment for

*T*HUS THE KIRTLAND TEMPLE BECAME, FOR MOST,

THE HIGHLIGHT OF THEIR SPIRITUAL AND RELIGIOUS LIFE.

THEY FELT AMPLY REWARDED AT ITS DEDICATION

AND THEREAFTER FOR THEIR SACRIFICE THAT WENT INTO IT.

—Dr. Ronald Esplin, Brigham Young University

Joseph and the saints, for he reported hearing the Savior say, "I have accepted this house, and my name shall be here."[26]

To the sorrow of many, even this season of spiritual strength was not enough to quell the spirit of apostasy that was growing in Kirtland. Mary Fielding described the city in 1837 as "a place where Satan has his seat."[27] Brigham Young, ever faithful to Joseph, said, "The knees of many of the strongest men in the Church faltered."[28]

"They believed Joseph had been a prophet," explains Dr. Ronald Esplin of Brigham Young University, "but they believed in some fashion that he had fallen. And so they couldn't leave it alone. They wanted to right the church. They wanted to rebuild it in their image of what it ought to have become, instead of what it was. Why were there so many? It was a high-demand religion. It required a great deal of sacrifice and dedication. And some folks tired of that and wandered off. Or some folks tired of it and tried to find another way of being Mormon without being so committed. But the other reason is that it changed. Joseph had a very ambitious program. Given the scope of the program, it could only be done step by step or, in Mormon terms, line upon line, precept upon precept. At every stage of innovation, somebody said, 'Wait, that's not what I bought into.'"[29]

Some expected near-godliness from Joseph. They wanted a pious prophet, not one who was sociable and engaging. Joseph Wakefield turned away when as a guest in Joseph's house he

You can never get back to the event itself. You can only get back to the testimony about the event. Unless you yourself were there, and if you were there but somebody else wasn't, you won't convince somebody else. So we are all in the traces business: What trace does something leave? That's how far back you can go, no further.

The traces we have in the case of the rise of the Latter-day Saints are the biography of Joseph Smith, the drama of the travails, the frailties, the temple left behind at Kirtland, Ohio, the people called in that name, the text of the Book of Mormon, the laws and regulations that he and his followers had that went with it. And you can take that as a total shape, that shapes the community, and you can push them back as far as they go. And then you can't go one step further—which may be one way of saying, "Had I been on the same hill, I wouldn't have seen what he saw." But I can make a great deal of sense out of his telling of what he saw.

—Dr. Martin Marty,
University of Chicago

watched the prophet "come down from the room where he was engaged in translating the word of God, and actually go to playing with the children! This convinced him that the Prophet was not a man of God, and that the work was false."[30]

Brigham Young remained one of Joseph's

1837, he directed trusted friend and apostle Heber C. Kimball to lead a missionary force to England to preach the gospel. Heber responded, "The idea of being appointed to such an important mission was almost more than I could bear up under. I felt my weakness and was nearly

Someone has observed that people can leave the church, but they can't leave it alone. And the worst persecutors of Joseph Smith were invariably those who had first been his associates and then had left his side and turned on him. Why this happened? I'm not sure. But it is not an unfamiliar phenomenon in human history.

—ELDER DALLIN H. OAKS, THE CHURCH OF JESUS CHRIST OF LATTER-DAY SAINTS

staunchest supporters. When he heard an antagonist bellowing about Joseph in the street he reported, "I put my pants and shoes on, took my cowhide, went out and, laying hold of him, jerked him around and assured him that if he did not stop his noise and let the people enjoy sleep without interruption, I would cowhide him on the spot, for we had the Lord's Prophet right here and we did not want the Devil's prophet yelling around the streets."[31]

Joseph wrote, "In this state of things . . . God revealed to me that something new must be done for the salvation of His Church."[32] In early June

ready to sink under it, but the moment I understood the will of my Heavenly Father, I felt a determination to go at all hazards, believing that he would support me by his almighty power, and although my family were dear to me, and I should have to leave them almost destitute, I felt that the cause of truth the gospel of Christ, outweighed every other consideration."[33]

"It was June Thirteenth . . . At nine o'clock in the morning of this never-to-be-forgotten day," wrote Heber's wife, Vilate. "Heber bade

RIGHAM YOUNG, an unfail-
ing friend and ally of
Joseph, joined the Church
in New York in 1831. After his baptism he
declared that he "wanted to thunder and
roar out the Gospel to the nations."[34] A
carpenter by trade, he became an avid missionary of the new religion. When he
moved his family to Kirtland in 1833, he,
like so many new converts, was destitute.
"If any man that ever did gather with the
Saints was any poorer than I was," he
recalled, "it was because he had nothing."[35]

In the heat of the controversy in
Kirtland, Brigham confronted some church
officials plotting to replace Joseph.
Brigham's history recounts what happened:

"I rose up, and in a plain and forcible
manner told them that Joseph was a
Prophet, and I knew it, and that they might
rail and slander him as much as they
pleased. They could not destroy the
appointment of a Prophet of God, they could
only destroy their own authority, cut the
thread that bound them to the Prophet and
to God, and sink themselves to hell."[36]

When the saints were later expelled from
Missouri, Brigham, as the senior apostle in
the Quorum of the Twelve, led them in a difficult winter flight to Illinois and safety.
From 1840 to 1841 he and eight of his fellow

apostles served missions to England. So
confident was Joseph of their contribution
that in August 1841 he announced "that the
time had come when the Twelve should be
called upon to stand in their place next to
the First Presidency." [37] It was with that trust
that Brigham stepped forward to lead the
church when Joseph was martyred.

adieu to his brethren and friends and started without purse or scrip to preach the gospel in a foreign land. . . . Sister Mary Fielding, who became afterwards the wife of Hyrum Smith, gave him five dollars, with which Heber paid the passage of himself and Brother [Orson] Hyde to Buffalo."[38]

The first baptisms came a month later. "At ten a.m [on July 30, 1837] they baptize nine members," Joseph reported. "When I heard of it, it gave me great joy, for then I knew that the work of God had taken root in that land."[39] Within eight months two thousand British citizens would join the new church.

This lifeblood of faithful converts did not translate into financial stability, however. To fund some of the needs of the burgeoning church and community, Joseph and his advisors established a bank, the Kirtland Safety Society. Financial failures were rampant in

the nation at the time; the Panic of 1837 devastated the economic status of communities across the country. When the Kirtland Safety Society was no longer able to redeem its notes in gold coin, they soon became worthless. Joseph's association with the company,

though he was not responsible for the daily operation, gave new rise to the chorus of "fallen prophet."

OF THE ESCALATING events, Joseph said, "The enemy abroad, and apostates in our midst, united in their schemes . . . and many became disaffected toward me as though I were the sole cause of those very evils I was most strenuously striving against, and which were actually brought upon us by the brethren not giving heed to my counsel."[40]

Tensions did not abate, and Joseph left the city in January 1838: "A new year dawned upon the Church in Kirtland in all the bitterness of the spirit of apostate mobocracy; which continued to rage and grow hotter and hotter, until Elder Rigdon and myself were obliged to flee from its deadly influence, as did the Apostles and Prophets of old. . . . As Jesus said, 'when they persecute you in one city, flee to another.'"[41]

The faithful trailed behind. That summer a mile-long wagon train moved slowly out of Kirtland and headed for Missouri. Hundreds of saints left behind their temple, their businesses, and their farms to follow Joseph to the farthest frontier of America.

"What the Lord will do with us I know not," lamented John Smith, Joseph's uncle, "altho he slay me I will trust in him. We are like the ancients wandering from place to place in the wilderness."[42]

6

WHEN JOSEPH fled Ohio, he did not put trouble behind him. In less than nine months, his plans for Missouri would collapse, his saints would again be forced from their homes by mobs, and he would be locked in a dark, dirty prison, his future uncertain.

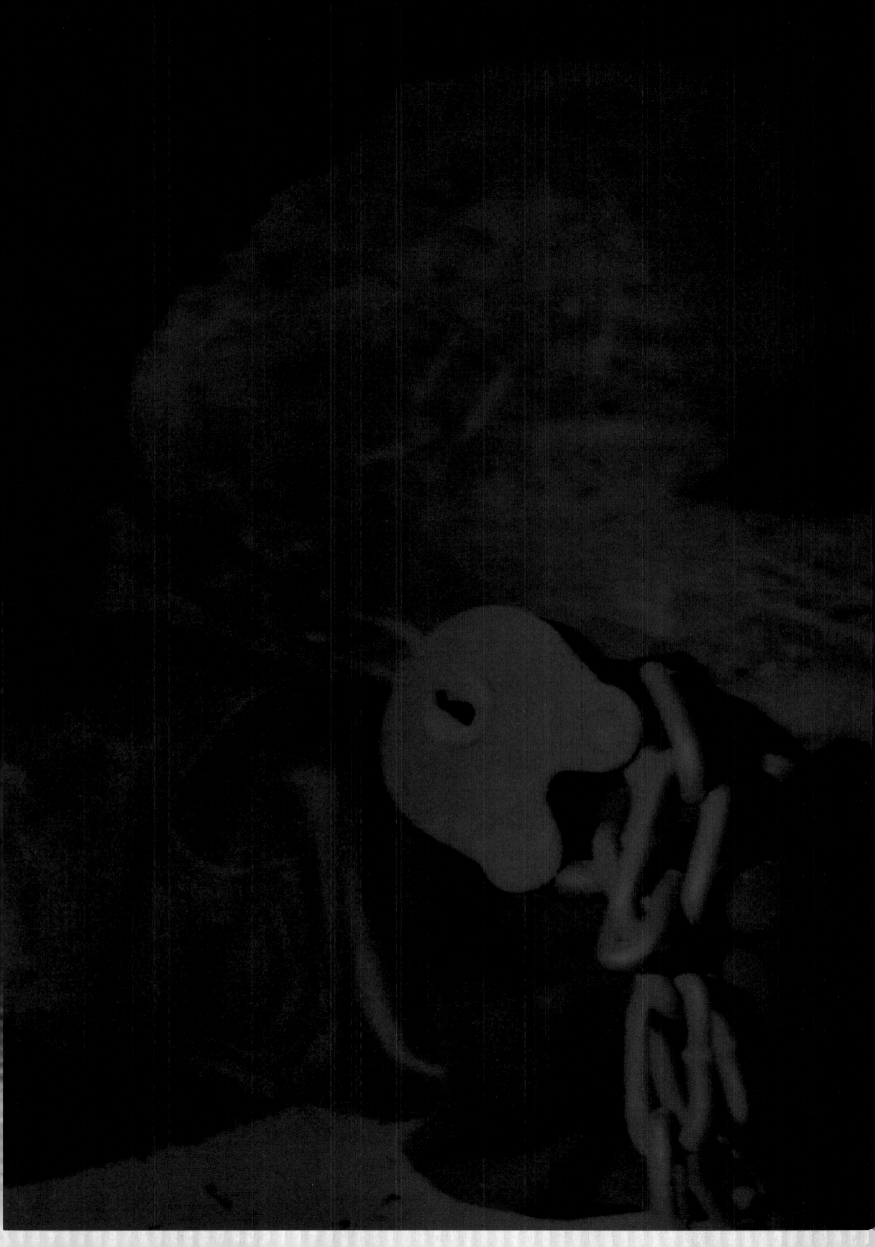

left all and retired into the back Country in the broad and wild Prairie, in the barren and desolate plains, and there commenced anew."[5]

Local church leaders David Whitmer, W. W. Phelps, and John Whitmer, who had shepherded the Missouri communities for the past several years, openly disagreed with Joseph and his policies and had fallen under a cloud of suspicion for financial dealings. They were asked to step down from their positions. Such disagreement was a pattern Joseph had seen before and would see again. Thomas B. Marsh, president of the Quorum of the Twelve Apostles, crossed over to side with Missouri antagonists, as did apostle Orson Hyde and some other prominent members. Marsh signed an affidavit stating, "The Prophet inculcates the notion, and it is believed by every true Mormon, that Smith's prophecies are superior to the laws of the land."[6] As Joseph observed, "Our difficulties and persecutions have always arisen from men right in our midst."[7]

Trouble loomed. "Those who cannot endure persecution, and stand in the day of affliction," Joseph would declare to the saints as a revelation, "cannot stand in the day when the Son of God shall burst the veil, and appear in all the glory of His Father, with all the holy angels."[8]

In an Independence Day speech, Sidney Rigdon denounced the enemies of the church, proclaiming that persecution would no more be endured. "We have not only, when smitten on one cheek, turned the other, but we have done it again, and again, until we are wearied of being smitten," said Sidney. "That mob that comes on us to disturb us, it shall be between us and them a war of extermination."[9] His remarks fed the fury against the Mormons.

Parley P. Pratt spoke with solemnity of the

danger: "War clouds began again to lower with dark and threatening aspect. Those who had combined against the laws in the adjoining counties, had long watched our increasing power and prosperity with jealousy, and with greedy and avaricious eyes. It was a common boast that, as soon as we had completed our extensive improvements, and made a plentiful crop, they would drive us from the State, and once more enrich themselves with the spoils."[10]

We peaceably left all and retired into the back Country in the broad and wild Prairie, in the barren and desolate plains, and there commenced anew.

– JOSEPH SMITH

Latter-day Saints were barred from voting in Gallatin, which led to altercations at Adam-ondi-Ahman and other Mormon communities. William Peniston, candidate for the state legis-lature, was particularly fierce in his opposition to the saints. On election day, worried that the Mormon vote would block his election, he shouted to a crowd, "The Mormon leaders are

The *Jeffersonian Republic* predicted battle. "Our ploughshares have been turned into swords in this quarter, and the Mormon War is the all-engrossing topic of conversation. Even politics is submerged in the deafening sound of the drum and the din of arms."[13]

In October, a clash at Crooked River claimed lives on both sides, including that of apostle

" OUR PLOUGHSHARES HAVE BEEN TURNED INTO SWORDS IN THIS QUARTER, AND THE MORMON WAR IS THE ALL-ENGROSSING TOPIC OF CONVERSATION. "

a set of horse thieves, liars, counterfeiters, and you know they profess to heal the sick, and cast out devils, and you know that is a lie."[11]

Joseph's assessment was bleak. "We had now, no hopes whatever, of successfully resist-ing the mob, who kept constantly increasing; our provisions were entirely exhausted and we being wearied out, by continually standing on guard, and watching the movements of our enemies; who, during the time I was there, fired at us a great many times."[12]

David W. Patten. Joseph said of him, "There lies a man that has done just as he said he would—he has laid down his life for his friends."[14] A few days later, in an unprovoked massacre at Haun's Mill, seventeen Mormon men and boys were murdered. Joseph paid tribute to the dead who "in consequence of their love of God—attachment to His cause—and their determination to keep the faith, were thus brought to an untimely grave."[15]

The last days of October, the Missouri mili-tia laid siege to Far West. Missouri Governor

Lilburn Boggs joined in the fray, declaring, "The Mormons must be treated as enemies and must be exterminated or driven from the state, if necessary for the public good. Their outrages are beyond all description."[16]

The Mormons were obliged "to shoulder [their] guns and stand guard night and day."[17] John Taylor described one confrontation: "The first thing we knew a flag of truce was seen coming towards us. The person bearing it said that some of their friends were among our people . . . and the mob wished these parties to come out as they, he said, were going to destroy every man, woman and child in the place. Joseph Smith, our leader, then sent word back by this messenger. Said he, 'Tell your General to withdraw his troops or I will send them to hell.' I thought that was a pretty bold stand to take, as we only numbered about two hundred to their thirty-five hundred. . . . They took the hint and left; and we were not sorry."[18]

The Prophet Joseph and a core of faithful finally agreed to a peace conference, only to be arrested and dragged to jail. "There was no alternative but to put ourselves into the hands of such monsters, or to have the city attacked, and men, women and children massacred," said Parley P. Pratt. "We, therefore, commended ourselves to the Lord, and voluntarily surrendered as sheep into the hands of wolves."[19] "The prophet Joseph was taken prisoner and we were obliged to lay down our arms," said Joseph Horne. "I obeyed this order because it was Joseph's counsel for us to do so, although I felt at the time I would rather have fought them."[20]

General John B. Clark reported to the Mormon people, "As for your leaders, do not once think—do not imagine for a moment—do not let it enter your mind that they will be delivered, or that you will see their faces again, for their fate is fixed—their die is cast—their doom is sealed."[21]

General Samuel D. Lucas of the Missouri militia, acting under authority of the governor, ordered the prisoners shot in the morning. Alexander Doniphan, the militia officer charged with the execution, defied the order, declaring firmly, "It is cold-blooded murder. I will not obey your  order. My brigade shall march for Liberty tomorrow morning, at eight o'clock; and if you execute these men, I will hold you responsible before an earthly tribunal, so help me God."[22]

Years later General Moses Wilson, a Missouri militiaman in whose charge Joseph had been

STEP BY STEP you could follow his decisions, the successes and the failures. At a dozen points it seems it's all over. The game's up. There's no way. And yet out of it comes a greater success and a growing movement that ultimately survives him, of course. And I marvel, again, at the fact that he could stand against the wind, against all opposition, and say, I know I had a vision and I know what God expects me to do.

—DR. RONALD ESPLIN, BRIGHAM YOUNG UNIVERSITY

placed for a time, described his prisoner's unusual presence: "He was a very remarkable man. I carried him into my house, a prisoner in chains, and in less than two hours my wife loved him better than she did me."[23]

The prisoners were shuttled from courtrooms to jail cells, first in Independence, then in Richmond, and finally in Liberty, where Joseph, Hyrum, and a handful of others were imprisoned for the winter. Joseph said of his plight, "All the world is threatening my life, but I regard it not, for I am willing to die any time when God calls for me."[24]

The guards in the Richmond jail taunted the prisoners with curses and boasts of raping and murdering the Mormons in earlier skirmishes. Joseph finally rose to his feet and rebuked them: "SILENCE, ye fiends of the infernal pit. In the name of Jesus Christ I rebuke you, and command you to be still; I will not live another minute and hear such language. Cease such talk, or you or I die THIS INSTANT!"[25]

Years later Parley P. Pratt reflected on that moment: "Chained, and without a weapon; calm, unruffled, and dignified as an angel, [Joseph] looked upon the quailing guards, whose weapons were lowered or dropped to the ground; whose knees smote together, and who, shrinking into a corner, or crouching at his feet, begged his pardon, and remained quiet till a change of guards. I have seen the ministers of justice, clothed in magisterial robes, and criminals arraigned before them in the Courts of England; I have witnessed

IF THE VISION of the infernal regions could suddenly open to the mind, with thousands of malicious fiends, all clamoring, exulting,

me in the year 1837

deriding, blaspheming, mocking, railing, raging, and foaming like a troubled sea, then could some idea be formed of the hell which we had entered.[26] —*PARLEY P. PRATT*

a Congress in solemn session to give laws to nations; I have tried to conceive of kings, of royal courts, of thrones and crowns; . . . but dignity and majesty have I seen but once, as it stood in chains, at midnight, in a dungeon in an obscure village in Missouri."[27]

With their prophet in jail, "There was but one course now open for the Mormons, and that was to make their escape with the utmost expedition," wrote John P. Greene, brother-in-law of Brigham Young.[28] Rather than disperse, the Latter-day Saints followed Brigham Young, senior member of the Quorum of the Twelve Apostles, in a ragged retreat to Illinois and safety. Lyman Wight described the evacuation: "I saw one hundred and ninety women and children driven thirty miles across the prairies . . . the ground thinly crusted with sleet; and I could easily follow on their trail by the blood that flowed from their lacerated feet on the stubble of the burnt prairie!"[29]

The exiles found refuge in Quincy, Illinois. The Democratic Association of Quincy called on the residents to "observe a becoming decorum and delicacy [around the saints], and be particularly careful not to indulge in any conversation or expressions calculated to wound their feelings, or in an way to reflect upon those, who by every law of humanity, are entitled to our sympathy and commiseration."[30] Sarah Rich, one of those banished from Missouri, reported, "[We] were glad of a resting place out

O F THE NINE *children Emma Smith bore, only four lived to maturity. Joseph later gave some resolution to the loss of infants when he said, "they were too pure, too lovely, to live on earth . . . [but] we shall soon have them again."*[31] *The children of Joseph and Emma were:*

ALVIN,
born and died June 15, 1828

THADDEUS AND LOUISA,
born and died April 30, 1831

JOSEPH AND JULIA
(MURDOCK),
*adopted twins, born April 30, 1831;
Joseph died March 31, 1832;
Julia died 1880*

JOSEPH III,
*born November 6, 1832,
died December 10, 1914*

FREDERICK
GRANGER WILLIAMS,
born June 20, 1836, died April 13, 1862

ALEXANDER HALE,
born June 2, 1838, died August 12, 1909

DON CARLOS,
born June 13, 1840, died August 15, 1841

STILLBORN CHILD
delivered in 1842

DAVID HYRUM,
*born November 17, 1844, five
months after his father was martyred;
died August 29, 1904*

of the reach of those who had sought our lives. We were truly a thankful and humble people."[32]

For Joseph's wife, Emma, the hasty exodus from Missouri was particularly wearing. With their four little children—Frederick and Alexander in her arms, Julia and Joseph III clinging to her skirts—she crossed the frozen Mississippi on foot in search of refuge. Under the folds of her skirt she carried two sacks containing Joseph's manuscripts of his Bible revisions.

Years later, Joseph's mother, Lucy, wrote of Emma, "I have never seen a woman in my life, who would endure every species of fatigue and hardship, from month to month, and from year to year, with that unflinching courage, zeal, and patience, which she has ever done. She has been tossed upon the ocean of uncertainty–she has breasted the storms of persecution, and buffeted the rage of men and devils, which would have borne down almost any other woman."[33]

In letters Joseph and Emma shared their trials and hopes.

"[Dear Emma] . . . I have been under the grimace, of a guard night and day, and within the walls, grates, and screeking iron doors of a lonesome, dark, dirty prison."[34]

"[Dear Joseph] . . . rolling rivers, running streams, rising hills, sinking vallies and spreading prairies that separate us . . . places my feelings far beyond description . . . but I still live and am yet willing to suffer more if it is the will of heaven, that I should for your sake."[35]

"Dear Emma I very well know your toils and sympathize with you if God will spare my life once more to have the privilege of taking care of you I will ease your care and endeavor to comfort your heart."[36]

IFE WAS NOT easy for Emma. She was the first lady of the church. She was always in the limelight. She carried a great burden herself. She was an exceptional lady of great capacity and great power and in many respects the strength of the prophet himself, who found in her companionship a much-needed strength to carry forward the great work throughout his entire life until the time of his death. She was left a widow while she was relatively young. I repeat, life was not easy for her. She bore it courageously and wonderfully and in my judgment was a remarkable woman.

—PRESIDENT GORDON B. HINCKLEY,
The Church of Jesus Christ of Latter-day Saints

"[Dear Joseph] No one but God knows the reflections of my mind and the feelings of my heart when I left our house and home, and almost all of everything that we possessed excepting our little children, and took my journey out of the State of Missouri, leaving you shut up in that lonesome prison. . . . I hope there [are] better days to come to us yet."[37]

The imprisoned church leaders were helpless to assist the fleeing Saints. Trapped in the Liberty Jail, they spent their days in a dim, damp cellar, the ceiling so low that the men could not stand upright. Their experiences in prison "would inevitably have proved fatal had not the power of Jehovah interposed in our behalf, to save us,"[38] said Hyrum.

Mercy Thompson accompanied her sister Mary, Hyrum's wife, to visit the prisoners. "We could not help feeling a sense of horror on realizing that we were locked up in that dark and dismal den, fit only for criminals of the deepest dye; but there we beheld Joseph, the Prophet, . . . confined in a loathsome prison for no other cause or reason than that he claimed to be inspired of God to establish His church among men."[39]

Historian Leonard J. Arrington identified one favorable effect of Joseph's miserable prison experience: "Liberty Jail was a 'wilderness' for the Prophet—a haven for contemplation and reflection in an unhurried manner with the Lord. A perusal of his journal suggests how very busy his life up to then had been—

While in jail, Joseph communicated with the members of the church in letters such as the following:

Liberty Jail, Missouri
December 16, 1838

To the church of Jesus Christ of latter-day Saints in Caldwell County, and to those who are scattered abroad, who are persecuted and made desolate, and who are afflicted in divers manners, for Christ's sake and the Gospel's. . . .

May grace, mercy, and peace be and abide with you; and notwithstanding all your sufferings, we assure you that you have our prayers and fervent desire for your welfare both day and night. We believe that that God who sees us in this solitary place, will hear our prayers and reward you openly.

And although our enemies seem to have a great triumph over us for the present, we most assuredly believe and know, that their triumph will be but short, and that God will deliver us out of their hands, notwithstanding their bearing false witness and otherwise. . . .

Dear Brethren, do not think that our hearts are faint, as though some strange thing had happened unto us, for we have seen these things before hand, and have an assurance of a better hope, than our persecutors, therefore God has made our shoulders broad, so that we can bear them: We glory in our tribulations, because we know that God is with us, that he is our friend, and he will save us. We do not care for those that can kill the body; knowing that they cannot harm our souls.

Joseph Smith, Jr.[40]

The winter cold seeped through the walls; the food was coarse, infested, and foul smelling; there was no bedding. When Joseph wrote Emma asking for a blanket, she replied that the mob, including former close associates of Joseph, had stripped their quarters of all they had, including the quilts.

traveling, meeting converts, spending time with curious visitors, counseling members, organizing and directing the affairs of the Church. The Prophet enjoyed people and was always with them. In the depressing surroundings of jail, the principal escape for Joseph and his companions during their confinement was into their own

Liberty Jail Clay Co Mo 1839 March 21th

Affectionate Wife

I have sent an Epistle to the church directed to you because I wanted you to have the first reading of it and then I want Father and Mother to have a coppy of it keep the original yourself as I dictated the matter myself and shall send an other as soon as posible I want to be with you very much but the powers of mobocray is to many for me at preasant I would ask if Judge Cleavland will be kind enough to let you and the children stay there untill I can l something further concerning my fate I will reward him well he will and see that you dono suffer for any thing I shall a little money left when I c my Dear Emma I very well know your toils and simpathise wit you if God will spare my life one more to have the privilege of takeing care of you I will ease your care and indeavour to cumfo you heart

minds and hearts. Biblical prophets were wont to go into the wilderness for periods of meditation and communion. Here the Prophet had uninterrupted time to ponder his course, to synthesize ideas, to formulate goals, and to communicate in an unhurried manner with the Lord."[41]

Liberty Jail gave Joseph the opportunity to sort out what had gone wrong, what needed to be done yet, and how to get it accomplished. Joseph left Liberty Jail with a very clear idea of what was left in his mission.

—Dr. Ronald Esplin, Brigham Young University

Joseph spoke of receiving encouragement from his friends and revelation from God even in his depressing circumstances. In a touching epistle expressing the pain of his own solitude, he wrote, "Those who have not been enclosed in the walls of prison without cause or provocation, can have but little idea how sweet the voice of a friend is; one token of friendship from any source whatever awakens and calls into action every sympathetic feeling; it brings up in an instant everything that is passed; it seizes the present with the avidity of lightning; it grasps after the future with the fierceness of a tiger; it retrogrades from one thing to another, until finally all enmity, malice and hatred, and past differences, misunderstandings and mismanage-

ments be slain victims at the feet of hope."[42]

The plea of his heart was expressed in the form of a prayer: "O God, where art thou? And where is the pavilion that covereth thy hiding place? How long shall thy hand be stayed, and thine eye, yea thy pure eye, behold from the eternal heavens the wrongs of thy people and of thy servants, and thine ear be penetrated with their cries?"[43]

Joseph described the answer to his pleadings as a revelation: "My son, peace be unto thy soul; thine adversity and thine afflictions shall be but

My son, peace be unto thy soul; thine adversity and thine afflictions shall be but a small moment

a small moment; And then if thou endure it well, God shall exalt thee on high; thou shalt triumph over all thy foes. Thy friends do stand by thee, and they shall hail thee again with warm hearts and friendly hands."[44]

One of those friends was his brother Hyrum. Five years older than Joseph, Hyrum was religious not only in his service to God but in his devotion to his younger brother. He said, "I am happy to say that my zeal for the cause of God, and my courage in defense of the truth, are as great as ever. 'My heart is fixed,'

humility of Christ, and I love him with that love that is stronger than death."[46]

After almost half a year in jail, the prisoners were granted a change of venue. The guards during the transfer were careless—perhaps purposely—allowing the prisoners to bolt. "We thought it a favorable opportunity to

I HAD BEEN *abused and thrust into a dungeon, and confined for months on account of my faith, and the "testimony of Jesus Christ." However I thank God that I felt a determination to die, rather than deny the things which my eyes had seen, which my hands had handled, and which I had borne testimony to, wherever my lot had been cast.* —HYRUM SMITH

and I yet feel a determination to do the will of God, in spite of persecutions, imprisonments, or death."[45] Since childhood the two had shared a bond that was a source of strength for Joseph. "I could pray in my heart that all my brethren were like unto my beloved brother Hyrum," said Joseph. "[He] possesses the mildness of a lamb, and the integrity of Job and in short the meekness and

make our escape,"[47] said Joseph of their flight.

The former prisoners "took [their] change of venue for the state of Illinois."[48] After ten days of traveling, they joined the saints who had been sheltered by citizens in the riverfront town of Quincy, Illinois. "I cried Lord what will you have me to do," said the newly released Joseph. "The answer was build up a city and call my saints to this place!"[49]

ᴵT IS IN ERROR TO PUT JOSEPH
AS A STAND-ALONE FIGURE.
IN JOSEPH'S GREATEST HOURS OF NEED,
HYRUM WAS THERE.

—*Elder M. Russell Ballard, The Church of Jesus Christ of Latter-day Saints*

7

In illinois, the newly liberated Joseph Smith took up the cause born years before in an illuminated grove in New York and reaffirmed in the dim shadows of Liberty Jail. He began by purchasing a sparsely settled swampland on a bend of the Mississippi and naming it Nauvoo, a Hebrew term meaning "beautiful city." ✳✳✳✳✳✳✳

HE PLACE was literally a wilderness," Joseph said of the site. "The land was mostly covered with trees and bushes, and much of it so wet that it was with the utmost difficulty a footman could get through, and totally impossible for teams . . . no more eligible place presenting itself . . . I considered it wisdom to make an attempt to build up a city."[1]

Wresting a new life from the marshes presented its challenges for the saints. Although they found respite from their persecutors, they suffered illness and disease in their new locale. "The Prophet says it is a sickly place," said Elizabeth Haven, "but [it] is made known to him that it shall be sanctified and be a place of gathering."[2] Elizabeth Ann Whitney remarked, "[We] were only just barely able to crawl around and wait upon each other."[3]

The accounts of Joseph healing "all the sick that lay in his path"[4] reflect a recurring theme of his ministry, "If you would have God have mercy on you, have mercy on one another."[5] On one occasion Joseph and Hyrum visited their uncle John, who was "delirious from the effects of the fever." Another member of the family expressed appreciation, "Their words comforted us greatly, as they said in the name of the Lord, 'you will be well again.'" Upon leaving the makeshift home in the side of a hill, Joseph placed his own shoes on his sick uncle's feet "and rode home barefoot."[6]

Wilford Woodruff, apostle and later fourth president of the church, recalled that Joseph "went among the sick lying on the bank of the river, where he commanded them in a loud voice, in the name of Jesus Christ, to rise and be made whole, and they were all healed."[7] Wilford said of another occasion of miraculous healing, "The words of the Prophet were not like the words of man, but like the voice of God. It seemed to me that the house shook on its foundation."[8]

But not everyone was healed. The harsh experiences of Missouri and Illinois had taken their toll on the Smith family, and on September 14, 1840, Joseph Sr. died. His funeral was "one of no ordinary importance," said Robert B. Thompson, Hyrum's brother-in-law, who acknowledged in tribute at the funeral service, "A whole society; yes, thousands will this day have to say, *A Father in Israel is gone.*"[9] Joseph expressed his own poignant loss, "He was the first person who received my testimony after I had seen the angel, and exhorted me to be faithful and diligent to the message."[10]

Harsh experiences of Missouri and Illinois took their toll. On September 14, 1840, Joseph Smith Sr. died.

"*The land was … so wet that it was with the utmost difficulty a footman could get through.*"

At first, the Mormons presented a pitiful sight at the horseshoe bend of this main water highway cutting through the continent. Reverend George Peck reported, "Some 200 miles above St. Louis, we saw on the Illinois side of the river a very singular encampment. Multitudes of people, men, women and children, ragged, dirty, and miserable generally, seemed to be living in tents and covered wagons for lack of better habitation. This strange scene presented itself along the shore for a mile or more. We were informed that they were Mormons who had recently fled from Missouri."[11]

The city would not remain so primitive. Only a few years later, Bostonian J. H.

> JOSEPH LAID OUT THE CITY WITH AMPLE SPACE FOR FLOWER AND VEGETABLE GARDENS, ORCHARDS, SUMMER KITCHENS, AND STABLES.

Buckingham observed, "In the history of the whole world there cannot be found such another instance of so rapid a rise of a city out of the wilderness—a city so well built, a territory so well cultivated."[12]

Nauvoo developed quickly. Joseph laid out the city in four-acre-square blocks, cutting each into a pattern of one-acre lots with ample space for flower and vegetable gardens, orchards, barns, summer kitchens, and stables. He reserved the bluff overlooking the Mississippi River for the building of a temple.

Up and down the streets shops opened for business: craftsmen, blacksmiths, tanners, coopers, and tailors offered their skills. Sawmills and grist mills, a match factory and a tannery, a gunsmith, bakeries, and even bonnet makers set up business.

Joseph ran a dry-goods store, though he was not much of a businessman. The procession of goods streaming out of his store was an indicator more of Joseph's largesse than of his business acumen. For example, James Leech and his brother-in-law, after arriving in Nauvoo, spent five or six weeks looking for employment. Their supplies exhausted, they went to see the prophet, though they were not yet members of the church. "He viewed us with cheerful countenance, and with such a feeling of kindness," James later recounted. "Said he, 'Can you make a ditch?' . . . He took us a few rods from the store, gave me the ring to hold, and stretched all the tape from the reel and marked a line for us to work by." The two went to work on the ditch, and when they had finished, "He came and looked at it and said, 'Boys, if I had done it myself it could not have been done better.' He led the way back to his store . . . picked two of the largest and best pieces of meat and a sack of flour for each of us, and asked us if that would do."[13]

Joseph settled his family in a small log house near the river. This "Homestead" would serve as church headquarters and as the setting for most official meetings in the early days of Nauvoo. A constant procession of callers and boarders kept Emma busy. Joseph helped with household chores, from carrying out the ashes to bringing in wood and water. He also plowed, planted, weeded, and harvested his farmland on the edge of town.

The city's growing economic vigor worried its neighbors. Newspaper comments suggesting that Nauvoo might "soon outrival any city in the West"[14] no doubt angered sponsors of competing communities. Businessmen in

 *There have been any number of such people, I think, who do feel that their mission has been divinely inspired, that they are directed to fulfill that mission. That gives them, I think, the kind of energy and purpose and determination by which I think they can do extraordinary things. And Joseph Smith did.* —DR. ROBERT REMINI, UNIVERSITY OF ILLINOIS AT CHICAGO

Warsaw to the south and Carthage to the east viewed the upstart Mormon community as not only a den for odd religionists but a threat to their commercial enterprises.

As historian Leonard J. Arrington explains, "From the outside, the Mormons, however destitute individually, must have looked like a fairly powerful economic bloc, with resources far exceeding those of any one individual. The perception of the Mormons as an economic threat—with respect to their control over their own trade and their effect on the land market—was repeated with variations in Ohio, Missouri, and Illinois. Neighboring towns were alarmed by the influx of Mormons into these different gathering places. Warsaw, Illinois, for example, had seen itself as a natural river port for the carrying trade, but suddenly found Nauvoo, twelve miles upriver, outstripping it."[15]

Word of Joseph's rising riverfront settlement spurred continued newspaper commentary on the prophet himself. James Gordon Bennett of the *New York Herald* wrote, "The Mormon movement is one of the most curious of the present age. It is inexplicable on the ordinary principles of philosophy. It is the beginning of a new dispensation, or it is nothing. There can be no mistake in Joseph Smith. He is a master spirit—and his ambition is to found a religious empire that will reach the uttermost ends of the earth. He has given the world a new Bible—and he is now busily engaged in founding a new kingdom of the faithful. . . . At this moment they have Apostles in England, France, and Germany, besides a deputation on the road to the Holy Land."[16]

Joseph did not intend to build a city for his flock alone. In a proclamation in concert with his counselors, Sidney Rigdon and Hyrum Smith, he issued an invitation, "Let all those who desire to locate themselves in this place [Nauvoo], or the vicinity, come, and we will hail them as citizens and friends, and shall feel it not only a duty, but a privilege, to reciprocate the kindness we have received from the benevolent and kind-hearted citizens of the state of Illinois."[17] Yet, for the most part, Nauvoo grew up as a one-religion town.

The Nauvoo Charter granted by the state of Illinois played a key role in the city's development. (Voting in favor of the document was a young legislator named Abraham Lincoln.) Pushed through the legislature by John C. Bennett, a bold, aggressive promoter who came on the scene in the early 1840s and quickly caught favor with Joseph, the charter gave Nauvoo unusually broad powers, including an independent court system and a university.

The charter also allowed Nauvoo to marshal its own military, the Nauvoo Legion. Joseph did not intend for the people to be without their own force in the face of any opposition. The Nauvoo Legion provided a sense of security to the citizens, but it was viewed as a threat by the rest of Illinois. An 1842 exhibition of the two thousand mounted troops

parading before dignitaries and officials from surrounding communities advanced a growing feeling that Nauvoo needed to be reined in.

The Nauvoo residents, on the other hand,

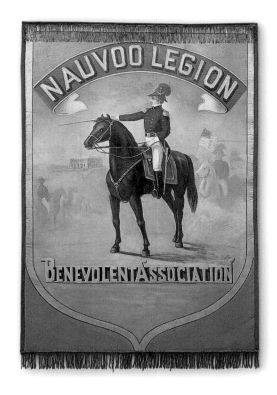

were thrilled with the show of strength. Said one woman, "Some of the most impressive moments of my life were when I saw the Nauvoo Legion on parade with the Prophet (then Gen. Joseph Smith) with his wife, Emma Hale Smith, on horseback at the head of the troops. It was indeed an imposing sight."[18] Young Mary Ann Winters described him as "grand as a leader . . . as he rode back and forth giving the commands of his office."[19]

Joseph held most of the posts of influence in

Nauvoo. He was the mayor, lieutenant-general of the Nauvoo Legion, a trustee for the University of Nauvoo, a subscriber to the Nauvoo Agricultural and Manufacturing Association, and publisher of a monthly newspaper, the *Times and Seasons*. He was also the chief justice. In one case, a man named Anthony had been accused of selling liquor in violation of the law.

never wanted him to go into the garden to work," said Emma, his wife, "for if he did it would not be fifteen minutes before there would be three or four, or sometimes a half a dozen men round him and they would tramp the ground down faster than he could hoe it up."[21] One woman convert said, "To him there were no strangers and by all he was known as the Prophet and a friend of

> I think the most significant thing about Joseph Smith's theology, or his teachings, is that he offered to the people of the frontier in the nineteenth century a knowledge of where they had come from, what the purpose of life was, and where they could go in the eternities and what they could become. And I think for those people it was tremendously significant to have a destiny, a divine destiny.
>
> —DR. ROSS PETERSON, UTAH STATE UNIVERSITY

To make it worse, he was charged with selling the liquor on the Sabbath. Anthony pleaded that he needed money urgently "to purchase the freedom of a dear child held as a slave in a Southern State. Joseph said, 'I am sorry, Anthony, but the law must be observed, and we will have to impose a fine.' The next day Brother Joseph presented Anthony with a fine horse, directing him to sell it, and use the money obtained for the purchase of the child."[20]

His people called him "Brother Joseph." "I

humanity."[22] Joseph's message was simple, "Remember God sees the secret springs of human action, & knows the hearts of all living."[23]

As in Kirtland and Missouri, Joseph remained intent on building Zion. "The building up of Zion is a cause that has interested the people of God in every age," he maintained. "Our children will rise up and call us blessed; and generations yet unborn will dwell with peculiar delight upon the scenes that we have passed through . . . the all but insurmountable difficulties that we have overcome in laying the foundation of a work that brought about the glory and blessing which they will realize."[24]

Joseph sought to establish a society whose every institution was infused with religious values and religious purpose. As Brigham Young described, "Joseph Smith . . . took heaven, figuratively speaking, and brought it

death."[26] The missionaries too were desperately ill. A gentleman who met them on the road asked "who had been robbing the burying ground—so miserable was their appearance through sickness."[27] "If you will go," said Joseph, "I promise you, that your family shall live, and you shall live, and you shall know that the mind of God is in calling you to go and

down to earth; and he took the earth, brought it up, and opened up, in plainness and simplicity, the things of God."[25]

In an ongoing rotation Joseph dispatched missionaries to England, Canada, Europe, and the islands of the Pacific to further the gathering. He sent Orson Hyde to dedicate the land of Palestine for its religious destiny. A brigade of his trusted apostles set out for the British Isles in 1839 to preach the gospel. They left behind wives and children "almost in the arms of

preach the Gospel of life and salvation to a perishing world."[28] The Elders, as they were called out of respect for the priesthood office they held, returned home in July 1841 to their families and an assembly of more than three hundred saints at the dock to greet them.

What began as a city of refuge became a magnet for the new converts. Between 1837 and 1846, Mormon missionaries baptized almost 18,000 in England. Of those, 4,700 crossed the Atlantic in the early 1840s to gather in Nauvoo or its outlying settlements. "In gathering to this land many shake out by the way, and others after they arrive," one woman concluded in a letter home to Britain.

PEOPLE EMBRACED MORMONISM BECAUSE OF THE FAILURES OF THEIR OWN RELIGIONS. IT WAS A RELIGION WHICH DID NOT ASK YOU TO MERELY COME AND SIT AND LISTEN TO SOMEONE ORATE. SOMEONE COMES ALONG WHO SAYS, "COME WITH ME AND DROP EVERYTHING YOU HAVE. MAKE A SACRIFICE. LIVE A DIFFERENT LIFE." SMITH IS OFFERING THEM SOMETHING THEY WANT. JOSEPH SMITH'S SUCCESS IS BECAUSE HE ASKED THEM TO GIVE AND TO GIVE MORE. PEOPLE WANTED TO GET RIGHT WITH GOD.
—*Dr. Robert Remini, University of Illinois at Chicago*

"Do not persuade any barren souls to come here—we want men of faith who can sacrifice their all for Christ's sake and the Gospel's."[29]

Emigrants from Europe came by boat to New York and then overland to Nauvoo, or to New Orleans and then up the Mississippi by riverboat. Joseph often appeared at the landing to greet the newcomers. "I could see one person who towered away and above all the others around him," recalled Emmeline Blanche Wells. "Before I was aware of it he came to me, and when he took my hand, I was simply electrified,—thrilled through and through to the tips of my fingers. . . . The one thought that filled my soul was, I have seen the Prophet of God, he has taken me by the hand." For years Emmeline did not speak of that first meeting, feeling it "too sacred an experience even to mention."[30]

"The gospel picks the big souls out of all creation," Hyrum said in commending those coming into Nauvoo, "and we will get the big souls out of all the nations, and we shall have the largest city in the world."[31]

I think anyone who studies the life of Joseph Smith, whether or not they believe he was divinely inspired, has to acknowledge him as a bold innovator. He was a man of immense power in creating new religious ideas and in attracting people to them. That I think is a simple historical fact.
—DR. RICHARD BUSHMAN, COLUMBIA UNIVERSITY

Orson Spencer characterized the new converts as "mostly from the working class of the community, from the United States and Great Britain and her provinces . . . rocked in the cradle of orthodoxy and liberty; accustomed to fatigue,

COME
WITH ME.
MAKE A
SACRIFICE.
LIVE A
DIFFERENT
LIFE.

privation and opposition."[32] Put simply, they were poor. "Those who have funds," Joseph explained, "have more generally neglected to gather, and left the poor to build up . . . the kingdom of God."[33]

While some converts from the East came by canal boat and stage, most of them walked. "We had come afoot, a thousand miles," recalled Jane James, a young convert of African descent who would later live in the Prophet's home and help with household tasks. "We lay in bushes, and in barns and outdoors, and traveled until there was a frost just like a snow, and we had to walk on that frost."[34]

Joseph approached one young man who had walked into town and engaged him in conversation. "He held me by the hand and pulled me forward until I was obliged to step up on the log. When turning his horse sideways he drew me step by step to near the end of the log, when, seeing that each foot left marks of blood upon the bark, he asked me what was the matter with my feet. I replied that the prairie grass had cut my shoes to pieces and wounded my

 UNQUESTIONABLY, THE QUALITY THAT MOST OF HIS FOLLOWERS SAW IN HIM WAS HIS ACUTE SENSITIVITY TO THE DIVINE AND HIS TENDER AND AFFECTIONATE SYMPATHIES TOWARD PEOPLE.
—DR. LEONARD J. ARRINGTON, FORMER LDS CHURCH HISTORIAN

When faced with treacher

was told that th

"Then I need have no fear

...nd mob attacks Joseph

...hildren had prayed for him.

...am safe," was his reply.

feet, but they would soon be alright." Joseph asked if others of the company were in the same plight and then said to a storekeeper, "Let these men have some shoes." When the merchant responded, "I have no shoes," Joseph replied, "Let them have boots, then."[35]

Many accounts praise Joseph's kindness and personal interest in others. He was particularly fond of children. When faced with treachery and mob attacks he was told that the children had prayed for him. "Then I need have no fear; I am safe," was his reply.[36]

Margaret McIntyre Burgess recalled: "My older brother and I were going to school, near to the building which was known as Joseph's brick store. It had been raining the previous day, causing the ground to be very muddy, especially along that street. My brother Wallace and I both got fast in the mud and could not get out, and of course child-like, we began to cry, for we thought we would have to stay there. But looking up, I beheld the loving friend of children, the Prophet Joseph coming to us. He soon had us on dry ground. Then he stooped down and cleaned the mud from our little heavy-laden shoes, took his handkerchief from his pocket and wiped our tear-stained faces. . . . Was it any wonder I loved that great, good and noble man of God."[37]

Others recounted buggy rides in the country and sleigh rides down the slope near his home to the river. Mary Ann Winters, out for a boating excursion with a large company, was caught up in listening to Brother Joseph speak. "My father sat opposite him, so near that their knees almost touched. I, a little girl, being tired and sleepy, my Pa took me in his arms to rest. Brother Joseph stopped speaking, stooped and took my feet on his knees and when I would have drawn them away, he said, 'No, let me hold them; you will rest better.'"[38]

Joseph never shed the negative images being painted of him in the press. However, when guests met him or heard him speak, they often changed their impressions. Washington politician Mathew L. Davis wrote to his wife, after hearing " 'Joe Smith,' the celebrated Mormon" speak, "He commenced by saying, that he knew the prejudices which were abroad in the world against him, but requested us to pay no

He was a man who enjoyed life. He wasn't a dour kind of man, he was a very happy kind of man, engaged in sports. He had a good time. But underneath all of that was a tremendous reservoir of spiritual power and strength. He spoke as a prophet. People listened to him. He could speak at great length on theological subjects to the enlightenment of his congregation. He was a man who lived near to the Lord, who could tap great resources of spirituality.

—PRESIDENT GORDON B. HINCKLEY, THE CHURCH OF JESUS CHRIST OF LATTER-DAY SAINTS

Even at meetings Joseph paid attention to the youth, as Harvey Cluff described: "At a Sabbath meeting in the bowery, myself and several boy playmates, were setting on the rude steps which led up the rostrum on which the Prophet Joseph Smith stood, discoursing with such power as to attract the attention of even boys. Policemen came and were driving us away, when the Prophet forbade them, saying, 'Let the boys alone, they will hear something that they will never forget.'"[39]

As much as his own people loved him,

respect to the rumors which were in circulation respecting him or his doctrines. . . . There was no violence, no fury, no denunciation. His religion appears to be a religion of meekness. . . . I have changed my opinion of the Mormons."[40]

Masonic Grandmaster Jonas attended the installation of officers of the new Masonic Lodge of which Joseph was a member. "During my stay for three days, I became well acquainted with their principal men, and more particularly with their Prophet, the celebrated 'Old Joe Smith,'" he commented. "Instead of

We want all honest men to have a chance to gather and build up a city of righteousness, where even upon the bells of the horses shall be written "Holiness to the Lord."[41] —Joseph Smith

Joseph Smith's view of women was very progressive for the time. They were hearty women, they had to be, because so many of them were coming with their husbands to the frontier. When he organized the Relief Society, he gave the women responsibility and a charge to act. That was quite a step forward at that time. He realized what they could accomplish, and the women rose to that occasion. The prophet could see beyond what they could do for the poor. He could see what they could do for women. When they were given that responsibility, they carried it out with fervor. —*Elaine Jack, former Relief Society General President, The Church of Jesus Christ of Latter-day Saints*

the ignorant and tyrannical upstart, judge my surprise at finding him a sensible, intelligent, companionable, and gentlemanly man."[42]

With the young men of the settlement Joseph enjoyed wrestling and a good game of ball. Enoch E. Dodge said of their amusements, "I have seen him run, jump, wrestle and pull sticks many times, and he was always winner."[43] Joseph was known for his strength in the wrestling ring. "He came to a large crowd of young men who were wrestling," friend Calvin Moore described. "Among the boys there was a bully from La Harpe. . . . He had thrown every one on the ground who took hold of him. . . . The man was eager to have a tussle with the Prophet, so Joseph stepped forward and took hold of the man. The first pass he made Joseph whirled him around and took him by the collar and seat of his trousers and walked him to a ditch and threw him in. Then, taking him by the arm, he helped him up and said, 'You must not mind this. When I am with the boys I make all the fun I can for them.'"[44]

In 1842 Joseph organized the women of Nauvoo into the Female Relief Society, with his wife, Emma, as president. He declared its purpose to be "that the Society of Sisters might provoke the brethren to good works in looking to the wants of the poor—searching after objects of charity, and in administering to their wants to assist; by correcting the morals and strengthening the virtues of the female community."[45] Emma told the women that their "duties to others were to seek

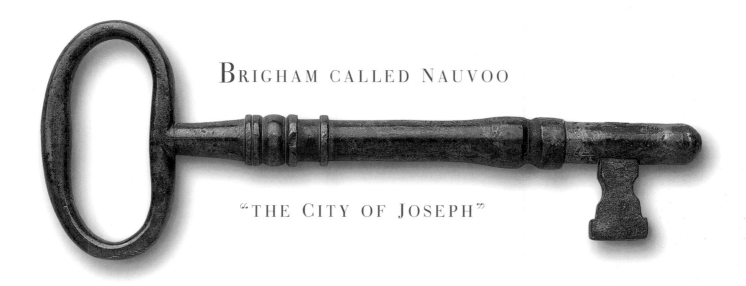

BRIGHAM CALLED NAUVOO

"THE CITY OF JOSEPH"

out and relieve the distressed—that each member should be ambitious to do good . . . deal frankly with each other . . . and be very careful of the character and reputation of the members."[46]

Joseph met often with the women, teaching them doctrine and principles. What began as a small organization of twenty quickly embraced hundreds. Eagerly they took to their charitable causes, meeting weekly to determine who was in need and to apportion the donations of money, goods, and services. They focused much of their work on providing clothing for the men working on the temple. Minutes of one meeting concluded with, "A union of feeling prevails through the meeting. All present manifested a disposition to do all in their power towards assisting the poor and in forwarding the building of the Temple."[47]

As Joseph fastened on what he called "the great work . . . now rolling on,"[48] he asked the saints, "Can I rely on your prayers to our Heavenly Father on my behalf . . . that I may be enabled to escape every stratagem of Satan, surmount every difficulty, and bring this people to the enjoyment of those blessings which are reserved for the righteous?"[49]

In many ways Nauvoo, like Joseph Smith, rose from nowhere. Its order and beauty, crafted from a malaria-ridden marsh, impressed visitors. Nauvoo was, according to Brigham Young, rightly called the "City of Joseph." "No other man, at this age of the world, has power to assemble such a great people from all the nations of the earth, with all their varied dispositions and so assimilate and cement them together that they become subject to rule and order. This the Prophet Joseph is doing. He has already gathered a great people who willingly subject themselves to his counsel, because they know it is righteous."[50]

8

IN THE EARLY 1840s Nauvoo stood on the threshold of power. Settlers pushing west clustered along the Mississippi, yet none were as organized or as driven to make a place for themselves as were Joseph and his people. A war cloud hung persistently over their labors. Said Joseph, with some urgency, "I shall not be sacrificed until my time comes; then I shall be offered freely."[1]

THE centerpiece of Joseph's Nauvoo was the temple. It was to be "considerably larger and on [a] more magnificent scale than the one in Kirtland."[2] The structure would be three stories high, 128 feet long, and 88 feet wide. Its design would include crescent moonstones, sunstones, five-pointed stars, a belfry, and a gold-crowned clock tower. "I have seen in vision the splendid appearance of that building illuminated," Joseph told the workers, "and will have it built according to the pattern shown me."[3]

Many saints tithed their time to its construction, yet still the temple drained the economic resources of the already struggling community. The *New York Sun* observed, "The building of the Mormon Temple under all the troubles by which those people have been surrounded, seems to be carried on with a religious enthusiasm which reminds us of olden times."[4]

In this temple the saints would be given what Joseph described as sacred priesthood ordinances necessary for eternal life. This holy work, the prophet said, had been revealed to him with

a promise, "Whatsoever you seal on earth shall be sealed in heaven; and whatsoever you bind on earth, in my name and by my word . . . it shall be eternally bound in the heavens."[5]

In anticipation of the temple's completion, Joseph administered to a selected few the temple ceremony that he called the endowment. "I spent the day in the upper part of the store, that is in my private office (so called because in that room I keep my sacred writings, translate ancient records, and receive revelations) . . . instructing . . . in the principles and order of the Priesthood. . . . All these things . . . are always governed by the principle of revelation."[6]

He also united families—husbands, wives, and children—in what he promised was a binding covenant for all eternity, called "sealing." Parley P. Pratt described the experience: "He taught me many great and glorious principles concerning God and the heavenly order of eternity. It was from him that I learned that the wife of my bosom might be secured to me for time and all eternity."[7]

As an expansion of his teaching that

The temple is the bridge between mortality and eternity. The temple, its doctrines, its significance were the culmination of Joseph's work.

—ELDER DALLIN H. OAKS, THE CHURCH OF JESUS CHRIST OF LATTER-DAY SAINTS

He united families—husbands, wives, and children—in a binding covenant for all eternity.

marriage could last through the eternities, Joseph introduced a few trusted friends to the added concept of a plurality of wives as practiced by Abraham and ancient prophets. What he termed the "new and everlasting covenant" included both monogamous marriage and plural marriage. The plural-marriage aspect sparked accusations of carnal lust and heightened antagonism against the Mormons.

The concept was troubling even to some of the faithful. Bathsheba Smith, a young Virginian recently married to Joseph's cousin George A. Smith, recorded her feelings about the new teaching: "I met many times with Brother Joseph and others who had received their endowments, in company with my husband. . . . I heard the Prophet give instructions concerning plural marriage. He counseled the sisters not to trouble themselves in consequences of [this law]; that all would be right—and the result would be for their glory and exaltation."[8]

Those closest to Joseph held fast to their commitment and loyalty, but even Brigham Young wrestled with the new revelation: "I was not desirous of shrinking from any duty, nor of failing the least to do as I was commanded, but it was the first time in my life that I had desired the grave, and I could hardly get over it for a long time. And when I saw a funeral, I felt to envy the corpse its situation, and to regret that I was not in the coffin."[9]

Joseph's position was clear: "It mattereth not whether the principle is popular or unpopular. I will always maintain a true principle even if I Stand alone in it."[10]

"What plural marriage did," says Dr. Jan

All we know is that everyone who was asked to live it found it a terrible shock. It stung them. And yet the most faithful of his followers went along.

—DR. RICHARD BUSHMAN, COLUMBIA UNIVERSITY

Shipps of Indiana University, "was make people commit to the church. It drew them in and made them commit. It had a purpose of creating a movement, of creating tradition. . . . Religious traditions come into existence through pain and exhilaration at the same time."[11]

Dr. Ronald Esplin of Brigham Young University adds: "Folks came eventually to identify Latter-day Saints with polygamy in such a way that even today, sometimes the first question a Mormon man is asked is, 'How many wives do you have?' And yet Latter-day Saints have not practiced polygamy for 100 years. It had a powerful impact in separating us, in drawing up boundaries, in making Latter-day Saints a people apart in a way that has persisted as a core part of our identity."[12]

Not all Mormons were able to demonstrate such allegiances. Some chose to leave Joseph's side because of his doctrines of the temple. Some of the most prominent were now at odds with the Prophet. Joseph described his own odyssey with the analogy, "I am like a huge, rough stone rolling down from a high mountain . . . all hell knocking off a corner here and a corner there . . . becom[ing] a smooth and polished shaft in the quiver of the Almighty."[13]

Dissension had stalked Joseph from the beginning. "When you joined this Church you enlisted to serve God," Joseph told ally Daniel

because I possess the principle of love. All I can offer the world is a good heart and a good hand. The Saints can testify whether I am willing to lay down my life for my brethren."[15]

He often discoursed for hours, rarely relying on a written text. He spoke in the tradition of the Puritans but with a revivalist element that kept the attention of his listeners, even the young ones. Eleven-year-old Alvah Alexander loved to listen to Joseph, saying, "No amusements or games were as interesting to me as to hear him talk."[16] His followers were consumed by thoughts and talk of the Millennium. Joseph

I GUESS PROPHETS HAVE TO SEE AHEAD. BUT WHEN YOU'RE IN THE MIDST OF A PROJECT, WHEN EVERYTHING SEEMS TO BE FALLING APART, WHEN THERE'S SO MUCH DAY-TO-DAY BUSINESS OF HOLDING THINGS TOGETHER—TO HAVE A VISION THAT CARRIES YOU BEYOND THAT, THAT'S A VERY DIFFICULT TRAIT OF A PERSONALITY, AND I THINK JOSEPH SMITH HAD THAT. I THINK HE WAS ABLE AMID TERRIBLY DIFFICULT CIRCUMSTANCES TO HOLD THAT VISION, IN FACT, TO KEEP ADDING TO THAT VISION, WHICH CARRIED HIM TO THE VERY END. —DR. LARRY MOORE, CORNELL UNIVERSITY

Tyler. "When you did that you left the neutral ground, and you never can get back on it."[14]

In funeral sermons, Sunday orations, weekly meetings, written epistles, and informal discussions, Joseph tried to prompt the people to draw closer to God. On one occasion he said, "Sectarian priests cry out concerning me, and ask, 'Why is it this babbler gains so many followers, and retains them?' I answer, It is

spoke as if that glory were in the reach of all. "If you wish to go where God is, you must be like God . . . for if we are not drawing towards God in principle, we are going from Him and drawing towards the devil. . . . Search your hearts, and see if you are like God."[17]

One whose faithfulness reached back to New York said of Joseph's teachings, "Even his most bitter enemies were generally overcome, if he

could once get their ears."[18] But a woman who had left the ranks of the church charged, "One needs a throat like an open sepulchre to swallow down all that is taught here."[19] Said Joseph, "I have tried for a number of years to get the

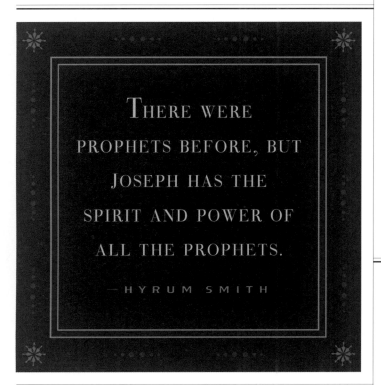

THERE WERE PROPHETS BEFORE, BUT JOSEPH HAS THE SPIRIT AND POWER OF ALL THE PROPHETS.

—HYRUM SMITH

minds of the Saints prepared to receive the things of God; but we frequently see some of them, after suffering all they have for the work of God, will fly to pieces like glass as soon as anything comes that is contrary to their traditions: they cannot stand the fire at all."[20]

Records show that Joseph delivered nearly two hundred discourses in Nauvoo. As Elder Dallin H. Oaks of The Church of Jesus Christ of Latter-day Saints explains, "I think the key doctrines that define his teachings are the nature of God, the apostasy, the necessity of a

restoration, the significance of priesthood authority, and the nature and purpose of life, and the destiny of men and women."[21]

Some saw Joseph taking his place among Abraham and the ancients. "This Joseph Smith is undoubtedly one of the greatest characters of the age," reported James Gordon Bennett in the *New York Herald*. "He indicates as much talent, originality, and moral courage as Mahomet, Odin, or any of the great spirits that have hitherto produced the revolutions of past ages."[22] Hyrum praised his brother, saying, "There were prophets before, but Joseph has the spirit and power of all the prophets."[23]

The doctrines Joseph preached were revo-

WE DON'T HAVE ISAIAHS AND EZEKIELS AND THE QUESTION OF WHETHER JOSEPH SMITH HAS MADE IT INTO A PANTHEON OF A PROPHET, RECOGNIZED BY PEOPLE OF OTHER TRADITIONS, IS CLEARLY NOT A SETTLED QUESTION. BUT I WOULD PUT HIM IN THAT TRADITION. —*Dr. Larry Moore, Cornell University*

lutionary for the day. "If the veil were rent today, and [you were to see] the great God who holds this world in its orbit, and who

upholds all worlds and all things by his power . . . you would see him . . . in the image . . . and very form as a man," Joseph told those assembled for the funeral of his friend King Follett in April 1844. "For Adam was created in

I've called Joseph Smith a popular genius because he was a person very unschooled, in a sense with very little formal education, and yet it was clear that his ability to comprehend religious ideas was enormous. And then his power to articulate them and to draw people to him was quite remarkable. I mean, he was magnetic, charismatic, whatever word one wants to use. It's astounding how, when he spoke in the name of the Lord, people took it seriously.
—DR. NATHAN HATCH, UNIVERSITY OF NOTRE DAME

the very fashion, image, and likeness of God and received instruction from, and walked, talked and conversed with him as one man talks and communes with another."[24] In this landmark discourse, Joseph addressed the character of God, the origin and destiny of man, the unpardonable sin, the resurrection of children, and his far-reaching love for all mankind.[25]

Thomas Sharp, business rival and editor of the *Warsaw Signal*, jabbed at the prophet

following the oration with an article titled "The Holy City": "Of course all the Saints and some of the sinners from the adjoining districts were in attendance. The number that was on the ground on this occasion is estimated at from 15–20 thousand—nearly all of whom were of the faith. Truly, one could think that so many fools congregated on one spot would disturb the equilibrium of the earth."[26]

I THINK ANY TIME THERE IS A PERSON WHO PROCLAIMS HIMSELF TO BE A PROPHET, AND TO CREATE A NEW ORGANIZATION, A NEW RELIGION, THERE IS A FEELING AMONG THOSE CONVERTED THAT THE MILLENNIUM WILL BE DELIVERED OVERNIGHT. AND WHEN THAT CRASHES ON THE REALITY OF EVERYDAY LIFE, THEN PEOPLE TURN ON THE PERSON WHO GAVE THE MESSAGE. –DR. ROSS PETERSON, UTAH STATE UNIVERSITY

Some in the church reached an impasse with Joseph over issues of doctrine. What had once drawn them to this American prophet—his distinctive claims and teachings—now repelled them. The *Sangamo Journal* carried a notice from a group of ten wishing to disassociate

themselves from Joseph and Mormonism: "We, the undersigned, feeling ourselves aggrieved by the conduct of Joseph Smith, and others of the leaders of the Church of Latter Day Saints—and feeling that we have been most scandalously imposed upon in matters and things of a Divine character, wish publicly to withdraw from said Church, and no longer claim allegiance thereto."[27]

FOR THE MOST part, the disenchanted simply abandoned the church and moved to other areas. But a core of believers felt bound to preserve Mormonism as they understood it rather than as Joseph was now teaching. They printed books, wrote articles, and spoke with derision of the Prophet Joseph. It was a pattern that repeated itself again and again.

William Law, second counselor to Joseph, was one such dissident. His position, shared by those who aligned with him in the spring of 1844, was clear: "Many items of doctrine, as now taught . . . considerate men will treat with contempt; for we declare them heretical and damnable in their influence, though they find many devotees." This group set out "earnestly seeking to explode the viscous principles of Joseph Smith."[28]

Nauvoo also drew resistance from its neighbors over its curious role as almost a city-state. The controversy reached even to the national press; the *New York Sun* reported in September 1843, "That Joe Smith, the founder of the Mormons, is a man of great talent, a deep thinker, and eloquent speaker, an able writer, and a man of great mental power, no one can doubt who has watched his career." But the paper questioned where Mormonism would end, warning: "A great military despotism is growing up in the fertile West, increasing faster, in proportion, than the surrounding population, spreading its influence around, and marshalling multitudes under its banner, causing serious alarm to every patriot."[29]

"I will assure you, that my soul, soars far above all the mean, and groveling dispositions of men that are disposed to abuse me and my character,"[30] countered Joseph. He consistently vowed that he was "bound to be a friend to all. . . . Whether they are just or unjust, they have a degree of my compassion & sympathy."[31]

THE FACT IS THAT WHEN PEOPLE HAVE DOUBTS, THAT THEN LAYS THE GROUNDWORK FOR WONDERING, HAS HE THEN BECOME A FALLEN PROPHET? SO THOSE PEOPLE INSIDE THE COMMUNITY WHO CONCLUDED HE HAD BECOME A FALLEN PROPHET THEN BEGIN TO ASK QUESTIONS. AND ONCE THEY BEGIN TO ASK QUESTIONS, THEY OPEN UP THE COMMUNITY FOR THE PEOPLE OUTSIDE WHO THINK HE'S A FALSE PROPHET OR THINK HE'S A PROFITEER INSTEAD. THEY OPEN UP THE WAY FOR PEOPLE ON THE OUTSIDE TO COME IN.
—*Dr. Jan Shipps, Indiana University*

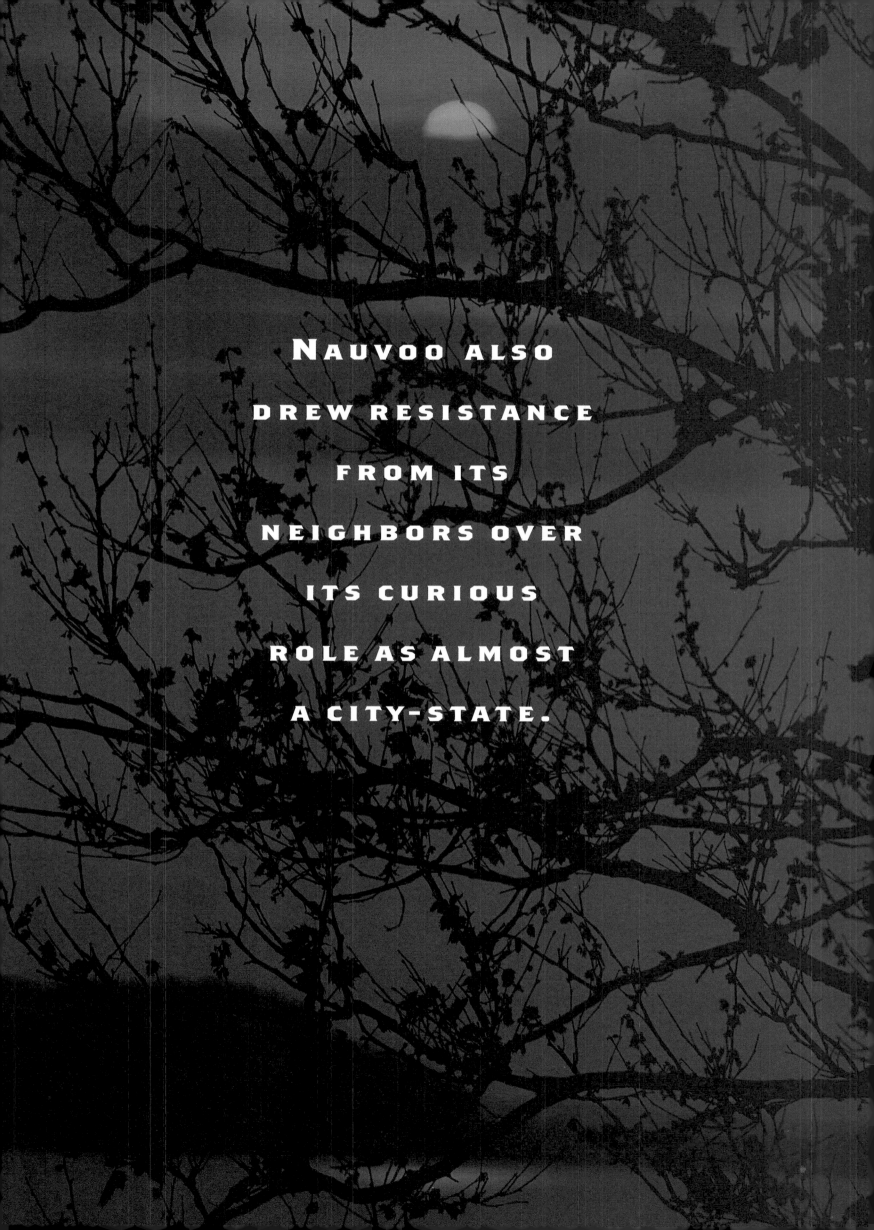

NAUVOO ALSO
DREW RESISTANCE
FROM ITS
NEIGHBORS OVER
ITS CURIOUS
ROLE AS ALMOST
A CITY-STATE.

In Illinois, Mormons were a force politically. Stephen A. Douglas was one who enjoyed their support and in turn befriended the church in early attacks. Joseph declared of Douglas, "We are willing to cast our banners in the air, and fight by his side in the cause of humanity and equal rights—the cause of liberty and the law."[32] Critics claimed that Joseph controlled the Mormon voting: "Let the ballot box, at every election where they have voted answer, and it will be found that they have voted almost to a man, with Smith."[33]

Joseph was becoming an increasingly powerful figure. In 1844 he announced his candidacy

for the presidency of the United States and dispatched able speakers to promote it around the country. This added fuel to the fire.

Said Joseph of the turmoil, "We contemplate

> STAND FAST, YE SAINTS OF GOD, HOLD ON A LITTLE WHILE LONGER, AND THE STORM OF LIFE WILL BE PAST, AND YOU WILL BE REWARDED BY THAT GOD WHOSE SERVANTS YOU ARE. —JOSEPH SMITH

a people who have embraced a system of religion, unpopular, and the adherence to which has brought upon them repeated persecutions. A people who, for their love for God, and attachment to His cause, have suffered hunger, nakedness, perils, and almost every privation. A people who, for the sake of their religion, have had to mourn the premature deaths of parents, husbands, wives, and children. A people, who have preferred death to slavery and hypocrisy, and have honorably maintained their characters and stood firm and immovable in times that have tried men's souls." He challenged the saints, "Stand fast, ye Saints of God, hold on a little while longer, and the storm of life will be past, and you will be rewarded by that God whose servants you are."[34]

In 1843 a faction of about 300 Illinois residents began searching out a way to repeal the Nauvoo Charter and blunt the growing influence of Joseph Smith. They regarded him not only as "the pretended prophet of the Lord" but as a power broker. Edson Whitney headed up a group of disgruntled neighbors, business competitors, and politicians who met in Carthage and renounced Joseph, stating, "Such an individual . . . cannot fail to become a

I feel tremendous admiration, love for the prophet Joseph Smith. My heart goes out to him, the things he suffered for this cause. He gave his life in testimony of its truth. From the time of his boyhood until the time he died, he was driven, he was hounded, he was persecuted, he was pursued. But he went forth courageously, adding a convert here, a convert there, organizing the church, establishing its doctrine, building it so that it would stand through the years that would follow. I have nothing but love for him. I reverence him, I respect him, I admire him, I honor him as the great American Prophet.

—PRESIDENT GORDON B. HINCKLEY,
THE CHURCH OF JESUS CHRIST OF LATTER-DAY SAINTS

most dangerous character, especially when he shall have been able to place himself at the head of a numerous horde, either equally reckless and unprincipled as himself, or else made his pliant tools by the most absurd credulity that has astonished the world since its foundation."[35]

Public sentiment reached a high pitch as the anti-Mormons at Warsaw and Carthage banded with dissenters, some of them former "one of the blackest and basest scoundrels that has appeared upon the stage of human existence," and his followers "hell-deserving, God-forsaken villains." The Nauvoo City Council retaliated by declaring the newspaper and its printing office a public nuisance and ordering the press destroyed. Mayor Joseph Smith declared martial law, but belligerence had flared beyond the borders of his influence. Illinois

Joseph breached one of the sacred lines in American political culture of his time. He joined the powers of church and state. He claimed to be a prophet to speak from God, to command men's consciences, their understanding of the world, and at the same time he liberally accepted offices of mayor, leader of his city. And for Americans, that combination of religious and political power was just explosive. They could not abide it. . . . I think that you do have to say that even though Joseph Smith trespassed on American sensibilities on freedom of the press, that did not license people to gun him down. —DR. RICHARD BUSHMAN, COLUMBIA UNIVERSITY

members of Joseph's inner circle. Thomas Sharp announced from the pages of his paper: "Joe Smith is not safe out of Nauvoo. . . . We would not be surprised to hear of his death by violent means in a short time. He has deadly enemies. . . . The feeling in this county is now lashed to its utmost pitch, and it will break forth in fury upon the slightest provocation."[36]

That provocation came quickly.

On June 7, 1844, William Law and others printed the first and only issue of the *Nauvoo Expositor.* Its columns accused Joseph of being Governor Ford intervened, an arrest warrant was issued, and Joseph was ordered to turn himself in at Carthage, the Hancock County seat. The charge before the court was treason.

From the *Warsaw Signal* came the passionate call to arms from Joseph's enemies, "War and extermination is inevitable. . . . CITIZENS ARISE, ONE AND ALL!!! Can you stand by, and suffer such INFERNAL DEVILS! To ROB men of their property and rights, without avenging them? We have no time to comment; every man will make his own. LET IT BE MADE WITH POWDER AND BALL!!!"[37]

Joseph Smith was not just a religious leader,
but mayor of Nauvoo and lieutenant general of its
military organization, the Nauvoo Legion.

Joseph at first refused the governor's warrant, saying, "We dare not come. Writs, we are assured, are issued against us in various parts of the country. For what? To drag us from place to place, from court to court, across the creeks and prairies, till some bloodthirsty villain could find his opportunity to shoot us. We dare not come, though your Excellency promises protection. Yet, at the same time, you have expressed fears that you could not control the mob, in which case we are left to the mercy of the merciless. . . . Sir, you must not blame us, for 'a burnt child dreads the fire.'"[38]

Time had run out. "There is no mercy—no mercy here,"[39] Joseph said of his options as he envisioned the governor's militia force rallying to overrun Nauvoo. "I love the city of Nauvoo too well to save my life at your expense," he concluded. "If I go not to them, they will come and act out the horrid Missouri scenes in Nauvoo. I may prevent it. I fear not death. My work is well nigh done. Keep the faith and I will die for Nauvoo."[40]

ON MONDAY, June 24, in company with Hyrum and some of his closest friends, Joseph began the twenty-six-mile journey to Carthage to submit to the latest warrants. This time there would be no generous judge, no legal loophole, no triumphant return to Emma and his family, his farm, or his service to God.

As he passed his fields on the edge of Nauvoo he paused, remarking: "If some of you had got such a farm and knew you would not see it anymore, you would want to take a good look at it for the last time. . . . I am going like a lamb to the slaughter; but I am calm as a summer's morning; I have a conscience void of offense towards God, and towards all men."[41]

His enemies were not willing to wait for a trial, broker a settlement or risk having Joseph somehow wrested from their grip. Joseph sensed their craving for frontier justice. To Emma and his family he wrote his farewell, "I am very much resigned to my lot, knowing I am justified, and have done the best that could be done. Give my love to the children and all my friends."[42]

A mob of two hundred made their move on June 27, 1844. Faces daubed with mud to disguise their identities, they stormed the jail. Three minutes later Joseph and Hyrum were dead.

> *Time had run out. "My work is well nigh done," said Joseph. "Keep the faith and I will die for Nauvoo."*

I AM GOING
LIKE A LAMB TO
THE SLAUGHTER;

BUT I AM CALM
AS A SUMMER'S
MORNING.

EPILOGUE

THE STORY OF Joseph Smith is not easily fashioned by names, dates, and places, nor have histories fully crafted his memory. As he himself boldly stated, "No man knows my history."[1] Much like Moses of old, he was driven to do God's will, come what may.

Said Joseph of his life's experiences, "Deep water is what I am wont to swim in."[2] Yet his message, even at the end, echoed his resolution: "No unhallowed hand can stop the work from progressing, persecutions may rage, mobs may combine, armies may assemble, calumny may defame, but the truth of God will go forth boldly, nobly, and independent, till it has penetrated every continent, visited every clime, swept every country, and sounded in every ear, till the purposes of God shall be accomplished, and the Great Jehovah shall say the work is done."[3]

Joseph Smith was a rugged individualist who "lived his life in crescendo."[4] He defied convention; he lived by conviction. This American prophet did not rise from one of the great New England universities or seminaries, nor did he preach from the pulpit of society or government. He was a farmer who spent his years on the edge of civilization yet always in the middle of controversy. He knew the struggles of making a living, the heartache of burying children, the weight of his ministry, the tensions created by believing what to his enemies was simply—unbelievable.

Joseph's influence with his followers was extraordinary. The persecution they shouldered, the journeys they endured, the sacrifices they made, the fervor they manifested in support of what he called the "kingdom of God on earth" is without equal in the religious history of this land. Those who disagreed with him over doctrine became bitter enemies. Those who feared his command over the burgeoning Mormon flock and its economic promise sought his downfall. Politicians courted his nod for the block of votes it would bring and then turned on him. It all came to an end June 27, 1844, at Carthage Jail.

"He lived great, and he died great in the eyes of God and his people; and like most of the Lord's anointed in ancient times, has sealed his mission and his works with his own blood,"[75] said John Taylor in tribute. Brigham Young echoed the sentiment: "I am bold to say that, Jesus Christ excepted, no better man ever lived or does live upon this earth."[76] Another time he said, "I feel like shouting Hallelujah all the time, when I think that I ever knew Joseph Smith, the Prophet."[77]

In less than three years following the martyrdom, ten thousand Mormons—men, women, and children—fled their country and their persecutors. They abandoned Nauvoo and their newly finished temple to trek thirteen hundred miles west to the Rocky Mountains. For the next twenty years, sixty thousand converts followed that trail of hope to a new Zion in the valley of the Great Salt Lake.

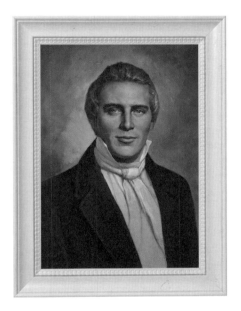

Perhaps Josiah Quincy, Harvard graduate and mayor of Boston, spoke with a sense of vision himself when he said of his visit with Joseph Smith in Nauvoo in 1844: "Joseph Smith, the Mormon Prophet . . . born in the lowest ranks of poverty, without book learning and with the homeliest of all human names . . . made himself at the age of thirty-nine a power upon earth . . . his influence, whether for good or for evil, is potent today and the end is not yet."[78]

HE LIVED GREAT, *and he died great in the eyes of God and his people, and like most of the Lord's anointed in ancient times, has sealed his mission and his works with his own blood.* —JOHN TAYLOR

NOTES

PREFACE

1. "Praise to the Man," in *Hymns of The Church of Jesus Christ of Latter-day Saints* (Salt Lake City: The Church of Jesus Christ of Latter-day Saints, 1985), no. 27.

2. Rachel Ridgeway Grant, *Young Woman's Journal*, vol. 16, no. 12 (December 1905), p. 551.

3. Bathsheba W. Smith, *Juvenile Instructor*, vol. 27, no. 11 (1 June 1892), p. 344.

4. Bathsheba W. Smith, *Young Woman's Journal*, vol. 16, no. 12 (December 1905), p. 549.

5. Alma P. Burton, comp., *Discourses of the Prophet Joseph Smith* (Salt Lake City: Deseret Book, 1977), p. 5.

6. Summary of remarks by Patriarch John Smith, 23 December 1894, in *Journal History*, 24 December 1894, p. 2 (Salt Lake City: Historical Department of The Church of Jesus Christ of Latter-day Saints, Archives Division. Hereafter referred to as LDS Church Archives).

7. Hyrum L. Andrus and Helen Mae Andrus, comp., *They Knew the Prophet* (Salt Lake City: Bookcraft, 1974), p. 154.

8. Mary Alice Cannon Lambert, *Young Woman's Journal*, vol. 16, no. 12 (December 1905), p. 554.

9. Hyrum L. Andrus, *Joseph Smith, the Man and the Seer* (Salt Lake City: Deseret Book, 1960), p. 10, quoting from *The Historical Record*, VII (January 1888), p. 476.

10. John M. Chidester, *Juvenile Instructor*, vol. 27, no. 5 (1 March 1892), p. 151.

11. Andrus and Andrus, *They Knew the Prophet*, p. 23.

12. Joseph Smith Jr., *History of The Church of Jesus Christ of Latter-day Saints*, ed. B. H. Roberts, 7 vols. (Salt Lake City: The Church of Jesus Christ of Latter-day Saints, 1932–51), 5:408. Hereafter cited as *History of the Church*.

13. Interview with Carol Cornwall Madsen for *American Prophet: The Story of Joseph Smith*, 19 May 1999.

PROLOGUE

1. *History of the Church*, 6:621–22.

2. *New York Herald*, 3 April 1842, as quoted in George Q. Cannon, *The Life of Joseph Smith the Prophet* (Salt Lake City: Deseret Book, 1964), p. 345.

3. *Teachings of the Prophet Joseph Smith*, sel. Joseph Fielding Smith (Salt Lake City: Deseret Book, 1977), p. 366.

4. Dallin H. Oaks and Marvin S. Hill, *Carthage Conspiracy* (Urbana and Chicago: University of Illinois Press, 1975), p. 20.

5. *History of the Church*, 6:602.

6. *History of the Church*, 6:622.

7. Lucy Meserve Smith, *Juvenile Instructor*, vol. 27, no. 15 (1 August 1892), p. 471.

8. William Hyde Journal, MS 1549, LDS Church Archives.

9. Maria Wealthy Wilcox, *Young Woman's Journal*, vol. 16, no. 12 (December 1905), p. 553.

10. Davis Bitton, *The Martyrdom Remembered* (Salt Lake City: Aspen Books, 1994), pp. 15–16; James Madison Fisher Journal, MS 1542, LDS Church Archives.

11. Bitton, *The Martyrdom Remembered*, p. 5; Aroet L. Hale Journal, MS 1509, LDS Church Archives.

12. Mary Alice Cannon Lambert, *Young Woman's Journal*, vol. 16, no. 12 (December 1905), p. 554.

13. Jane James, *Young Woman's Journal*, vol. 16, no. 12 (December 1905), pp. 552–53.

14. Eliza R. Snow, "Generals Joseph Smith and Hyrum Smith," in *Poems by Eliza R. Snow* (Nauvoo, Ill.: n.p., 1844), pp. 142–45; *Times and Seasons*, vol. 5, no. 12 (1 July 1844), p. 575.

15. *History of the Church*, 6:627.

16. E. Cecil McGavin, *Nauvoo the Beautiful* (Salt Lake City: Bookcraft, 1972), p. 148.

17. Bitton, *The Martyrdom Remembered*, p. 7.

18. Parley P. Pratt, *Autobiography of Parley P. Pratt* (Salt Lake City: Deseret Book, 1985 ed.), p. 292.

19. Bitton, *The Martyrdom Remembered*, pp. 14–15; Heber C. Kimball Journal, 9 July 1844, LDS Church Archives.

20. Leonard J. Arrington and Davis Bitton, *The Mormon Experience* (Urbana and Chicago: University of Illinois Press, 1992), p. 82; Brigham Young to Vilate Young, 11 August 1844, LDS Church Archives.

21. John Telford, Susan Easton Black, and Kim C Averett, *Nauvoo* (Salt Lake City: Deseret Book, 1997), p. 68; *New York Herald*, 8 July 1844.

22. McGavin, *Nauvoo the Beautiful*, p. 153.

23. Rev. William G. Brownlow, *Jonesborough Whig*, 24 July 1844; reprinted in *Warsaw Signal*, 19 February 1845.

24. Reprinted in *Nauvoo Neighbor*, vol. 2, no. 11 (10 July 1844), p. 3.

25. *History of the Church*, 7:180.

26. *History of the Church*, 6:3.

27. Dix W. Price, "I Met Joseph Smith," *Speeches of the Year*, 1962 (Provo, Utah: Brigham Young University, 1962); quoting from *New York Weekly Herald*, 12 July 1844.

28. "Letter from a highly respectable gentleman to his friend in Nauvoo," reprinted in *Nauvoo Neighbor*, vol. 2, no. 15 (7 August 1844), p. 2.

29. *History of the Church*, 7:37.

30. Josiah Quincy, *Figures of the Past* (Boston: Roberts Brothers, 1884), p. 376.

1 FROM THESE ROOTS

1. Interview with Martin Marty for *American Prophet: The Story of Joseph Smith*, 10 December 1998.

2. *Teachings of the Prophet Joseph Smith*, sel. Joseph Fielding Smith (Salt Lake City: Deseret Book, 1977), p. 179.

3. As quoted in interview with Leonard J. Arrington for *American Prophet: The Story of Joseph Smith*, 20 October 1998.

4. Benjamin Franklin, urging that prayer be offered during Constitutional Convention, 28 June 1787; as quoted in David O. McKay, *Man May Know for Himself*, comp. Clare Middlemiss (Salt Lake City: Deseret Book, 1967), p. 355.

5. Interview with Martin Marty, 10 December 1998.

6. Lucy Mack Smith, *History of Joseph Smith by His Mother*, ed. Preston Nibley (Salt Lake City: Bookcraft, 1954), p. 46.

7. As cited in Richard L. Bushman, *Joseph Smith and the Beginnings of Mormonism* (Urbana and Chicago: University of Illinois Press, 1984), p. 20.

8. Richard Lloyd Anderson, *Joseph Smith's New England Heritage* (Salt Lake City: Deseret Book, 1971), pp. 124–29.

9. *Journal of Discourses* 26 vols. (London: Latter-day Saints' Book Depot, 1856–86), 7:289–90. Hereafter cited as *Journal of Discourses*.

10. Lucy Mack Smith, *History of Joseph Smith*, p. 67.

11. Ibid.

12. Ibid., p. 55.

13. Ibid., p. 57.

14. Ibid., p. 63.

15. As cited in Milton V. Backman Jr., "Defender of the First Vision," in Larry C. Porter, Milton V. Backman Jr., and Susan Easton Black, eds., *Regional Studies in Latter-day Saint Church History—New York* (Provo, Utah: Dept. of Church History and Doctrine, Brigham Young University, 1992), p. 38.

16. Lucy Mack Smith, *History of Joseph Smith*, p. 63.

17. Dean C. Jessee, ed., *The Personal Writings of Joseph Smith* (Salt Lake City: Deseret Book, 1984), p. 4.

18. "William Smith Interview," *Deseret Evening News*, 20 January 1894, 28:11.

19. As cited in James B. Allen and Glen M. Leonard, *The Story of the Latter-day Saints* (Salt Lake City: Deseret Book, 1992), p. 25.

20. Lucy Mack Smith, *History of Joseph Smith*, p. 65.

21. As cited in Donna Hill, *Joseph Smith, the First Mormon* (Garden City, NY: Doubleday and Co., 1977), p. 43.

22. Donald L. Enders, "The Sacred Grove," *Ensign*, April 1990, p. 16.

2 LO HERE, LO THERE

1. Interview with Gordon Wood for *American Prophet: The Story of Joseph Smith*, 9 December 1998.

2. Lucy Mack Smith, *History of Joseph Smith by His Mother*, ed. Preston Nibley (Salt Lake City: Bookcraft, 1954), p. 66.

3. Lucy Mack Smith, *Biographical Sketches of Joseph Smith the Prophet and His Progenitors for Many Generations* (Liverpool: Published for Orson Pratt by S.W.Richards, 1853), p. 84.

4. Dean C. Jessee, ed., *The Personal Writings of Joseph Smith* (Salt Lake City: Deseret Book, 1984), p. 4.

5. *History of the Church*, 1:3.

6. Jessee, *Personal Writings of Joseph Smith*, p. 75.

7. Donna Hill, *Joseph Smith, the First Mormon* (Garden City, NY: Doubleday and Co., 1977), p. 49; Milton V. Backman Jr., *Joseph Smith's First Vision* (Salt Lake City: Bookcraft, 1971), pp. 109–10.

8. Dean C. Jessee, ed., *The Papers of Joseph Smith: Autobiographical and Historical Writings*, 2 vols. (Salt Lake City: Deseret Book, 1989), 1:5.

9. Milton V. Backman Jr., *Eyewitness Accounts of the Restoration* (Orem, Utah: Grandin Book Co., 1983), p. 23.

10. Lucy Mack Smith, *History of Joseph Smith*, p. 90.

11. Jessee, *Personal Writings of Joseph Smith*, p.198.

12. James 1:5.

13. Jessee, *Personal Writings of Joseph Smith*, p. 199.

14. Ibid.

15. Ibid.

16. Ibid.

17. Ibid., pp. 199–200.

18. Ibid., p. 213.

19. Jessee, *Papers of Joseph Smith*, 1: 273–74.

20. Ibid., p. 274.

21. Ibid., p. 275.

22. Ibid.

23. Jessee, *Personal Writings of Joseph Smith*, pp. 200–201.

24. Interview with Dallin H. Oaks for *American Prophet: The Story of Joseph Smith*, 7 December 1998.

25. Lucy Mack Smith, *History of Joseph Smith*, p. 68.

26. Jessee, *Papers of Joseph Smith*, 1: 275.

27. Andrew F. Ehat and Lyndon W. Cook, comps., *The Words of Joseph Smith: The Contemporary Account of the Nauvoo Discourses of the Prophet Joseph* (Orem, Utah: Grandin Book Co., 1993), p. 253.

28. *History of the Church*, 1:9.

29. Jessee, *Papers of Joseph Smith*, 1: 276.

30. Ibid., pp. 276–77.

31. Ibid., p. 277.

32. Jessee, *Personal Writings of Joseph Smith*, pp. 205–6.

33. Interview with M. Russell Ballard for *American Prophet: The Story of Joseph Smith*, 7 December 1998.

34. Jessee, *Papers of Joseph Smith*, 1:282.

35. Lucy Mack Smith, *History of Joseph Smith*, p. 81.

36. Ibid.

37. "Another Testimony: Statement of William Smith, Concerning Joseph the Prophet," *Deseret Evening News*, 20 January 1894, p. 11.

38. Lucy Mack Smith, *History of Joseph Smith*, p. 83.

39. Ibid., p. 82.

40. Ibid., p. 88.

41. Jessee, *Personal Writings of Joseph Smith*, p. 531.

42. Susan Easton Black, "Isaac Hale: Antagonist of Joseph Smith," in Larry C. Porter, Milton V. Backman Jr., and Susan Easton Black, eds., *Regional Studies in Latter-day Saint Church History—New York* (Provo, Utah: Dept. of Church History and Doctrine, Brigham Young University, 1992), p. 100.

43. Liz Lemon Swindle and Susan Easton Black, *Joseph Smith: Impressions of a Prophet* (Salt Lake City: Deseret Book, 1998), p. 27; "Last Testimony of Sister Emma," *The Saints Herald* 26 (1 October 1879): 289–90, as cited in Backman, *Eyewitness Accounts*, p. 54.

3 AN ANCIENT RECORD

1. Dean C. Jessee, "Joseph Knight's Recollection of Early Mormon History," *Brigham Young University Studies*, vol. 17, no. 1 (Autumn 1976), pp. 32–33.

2. Lucy Mack Smith, *History of Joseph Smith by His Mother*, ed. Preston Nibley (Salt Lake City: Bookcraft, 1954), p. 104.

3. Ibid., p. 110.

4. Dean C. Jessee, ed., *The Personal Writings of Joseph Smith* (Salt Lake City: Deseret Book, 1984), pp. 214–215.

5. Dean C. Jessee, ed., *The Papers of Joseph Smith: Autobiographical and Historical Writings*, 2 vols. (Salt Lake City: Deseret Book, 1989), 1:431; Letter to John Wentworth, *Times and Seasons* 3 (1 March 1842): 706–10.

6. Lucy Mack Smith, *Biographical Sketches of Joseph Smith the Prophet and His Progenitors for Many Generations* (Liverpool: Published for Orson Pratt by S.W.Richards, 1853), p. 116.

7. Donna Hill, *Joseph Smith, the First Mormon* (Garden City, NY: Doubleday and Co., 1977), p. 72; spelling and punctuation corrected.

8. Lucy Mack Smith, *History of Joseph Smith*, p. 106.

9. Ibid., p. 108.

10. Ibid., p. 109.

11. The Susquehanna Register (Montrose), 1 May 1834, as cited in Larry C. Porter, *A Study of the Origins of The Church of Jesus Christ of Latter-day Saints in the States of New York and Pennsylvania, 1816–1831*, dissertation presented to the Department of Church History and Doctrine, Brigham Young University, 1971, p. 132.

12. Ibid.

13. Interview of Emma Smith Bidamon by Nels Madson and Parley P. Pratt, Jr., 1877, LDS Church Archives.

14. Statement of Emma Smith to her son Joseph Smith III, cited in *The Saints Herald*, 26 (1 October 1879): 290.

15. "Last Testimony of Sister Emma," *The Saints Herald*, 26 (1 October 1879): 290; as cited in Milton V. Backman Jr., *Eyewitness Accounts of the Restoration* (Orem, Utah: Grandin Book Co., 1983), p. 127.

16. B. H. Roberts, ed., *A Comprehensive History of The Church of Jesus Christ of Latter-day Saints*, 6 vols. (Salt Lake City: Deseret News Press, 1930), 1:102.

17. Lucy Mack Smith, *History of Joseph Smith*, p. 128.

18. Ibid., p. 129.

19. Doctrine and Covenants 3:10.

20. *Latter Day Saints' Messenger and Advocate*, October 1834, p. 15.

21. Hill, *Joseph Smith, the First Mormon*, p. 85; Joseph Knight Sr. ms., LDS Church Archives.

22. *History of the Church*, 1:44.

23. *Latter Day Saints' Messenger and Advocate*, October 1835, p. 201.

24. Edwin F. Parry, *Stories about Joseph Smith the Prophet* (Salt Lake City: Deseret News Press, 1934), pp. 66–67.

25. Richard L. Bushman, *Joseph Smith and the Beginnings of Mormonism* (Urbana and Chicago: University of Illinois Press, 1984), p. 104; David Whitmer, "Address to All Believers," p. 30.

26. Book of Mormon, "The Testimony of Three Witnesses," p. viii.

27. Journal of Reuben Miller, October 1848, LDS Church Archives.

28. Lyndon W. Cook, ed., *David Whitmer Interviews, a Restoration Witness* (Orem, Utah: Grandin Book Co., 1991), p. xiv.

29. "A Proclamation," appended to an interview with a correspondent of the *Chicago Times* (Richmond, Missouri, 14 October 1881), originally published in *Chicago Times*, 17 October 1881, and reprinted in Cook, *David Whitmer Interviews*, p. 79.

30. Lucy Mack Smith, *Biographical Sketches*, p. 165.

31. See Bushman, *Joseph Smith and the Beginnings of Mormonism*, p. 103; quoting from *Deseret Evening News*, 16 November 1878.

32. John Gilbert, Typescript, Brigham Young University, p. 2.

33. Ibid., p. 3.

34. *History of the Church*, 4:461.

35. Larry Porter, "The Book of Mormon: Historical Setting for Its Translation and Publication," in Susan Easton Black and Charles D. Tate Jr., eds., *Joseph Smith, The Prophet, The Man: Selected papers from the Joseph Smith Symposium*, 22 February 1992, p. 59.

36. *Journal of Discourses*, 8:38.

37. *Latter Day Saints' Messenger and Advocate*, September 1835, p. 178.

38. Leonard J. Arrington and Davis Bitton, *The Mormon Experience* (Urbana and Chicago: University of Illinois Press, 1992), p. 32; Orson Spencer, *Letter Exhibiting the Most Prominent Doctrines of the Church of Jesus Christ of Latter-day Saints* (Liverpool, England, 1848), pp. 8–9.

39. Interview with Grant McMurray for *American Prophet: The Story of Joseph Smith*, 18 December 1998.

40. As cited in Francis Kirkham, *A New Witness for Christ in America: The Book of Mormon*, 2 vols. [Salt Lake City: Utah Printing Co., 1967], 1:150.

41. As cited in Pearson H. Corbett, *Hyrum Smith–Patriarch* (Salt Lake City: Deseret Book, 1963), p. 60; *Palmyra Reflector*, 20 June 1830.

42. As cited in Bushman, *Joseph Smith and the Beginnings of Mormonism*, p. 112.

43. Ibid., p. 126.

44. Ibid., p. 111.

45. Ibid.

46. Interview with Mario DePillis for *American Prophet: The Story of Joseph Smith*, 8 December 1998.

47. *Times and Seasons* 4 (December 1842):22.

4 THE KINGDOM OF GOD ON EARTH

1. Doctrine and Covenants 21:1.

2. Dean C. Jessee, "Joseph Knight's Recollection of Early Mormon History," *Brigham Young University Studies*, vol. 17, no. 1 (Autumn 1976), p. 37; spelling and punctuation corrected.

3. *Teachings of the Prophet Joseph Smith*, sel. Joseph Fielding Smith (Salt Lake City: Deseret Book, 1977), p. 233.

4. Doctrine and Covenants 77:11.

5. Book of Mormon, Mosiah 23:17.

6. Doctrine and Covenants 13:1.

7. *History of the Church*, 1:42–43.

8. Pearl of Great Price, Joseph Smith—History 1:68.

9. *Latter Day Saints' Messenger and Advocate*, October 1834, pp. 15–16.

10. Lucy Mack Smith, *History of Joseph Smith by His Mother*, ed. Preston Nibley (Salt Lake City: Bookcraft, 1954), p. 168.

11. *History of the Church*, 1:78.

12. Parley P. Pratt, *Autobiography of Parley P. Pratt* (Salt Lake City: Deseret Book, 1985 ed.), p. 36.

13. Davis Bitton, "Kirtland as a Center of Missionary Activity 1830–1838," *Brigham Young University Studies*, vol. 11, no. 4 (Summer 1971), p. 505.

14. As cited in Donna Hill, *Joseph Smith, the First Mormon* (Garden City, NY: Doubleday and Co., 1977), p. 121.

15. As cited in Richard L. Bushman, *Joseph Smith and the Beginnings of Mormonism* (Urbana and Chicago: University of Illinois Press, 1984), p. 121.

16. As cited in Leonard J. Arrington and Davis Bitton, *The Mormon Experience* (Urbana and Chicago: University of Illinois Press, 1992), pp. 29–30.

17. *History of the Church*, 1:86.

18. Bushman, *Joseph Smith and the Beginnings of Mormonism*, p. 165.

19. As cited in Larry C. Porter, Milton V. Backman Jr., and Susan Easton Black, eds., *Regional Studies in Latter-day Saint Church History—New York* (Provo, Utah: Dept. of Church History and Doctrine, Brigham Young University, 1992), p. 161.

20. "Newel Knight's Journal," *Scraps of Biography* (Salt Lake City: Juvenile Instructor Office, 1883), 10:68.

21. *History of the Church*, 4:272.

22. Karl Ricks Anderson, *Joseph Smith's Kirtland* (Salt Lake City: Deseret Book, 1989), p. 14; History of Geauga and Lake counties, Ohio, p. 248.

23. Louisa Y. Littlefield, "Recollections of the Prophet Joseph Smith," *Juvenile Instructor*, vol. 27, no. 1 (1 January 1892), p. 24.

24. Writings of Early Latter-day Saints, "A Biographical Sketch of the Life of *Jonathan Crosby Written by Himself*, p. 14, Utah State Historical Society, Salt Lake City, Utah.

25. Marvin S. Hill, "Joseph Smith the Man: Some Reflections on a Subject of Controversy," *Brigham Young University Studies*, vol. 21, no. 2 (Spring 1981), p. 186.

26. *History of the Church*, 1:215–16, fn.

27. *History of the Church*, 1: 245.

28. Doctrine and Covenants 76:19–23

29. Philo Dibble, *Juvenile Instructor*, vol. 27, no. 10 (15 May 1892), pp. 303–4.

30. *Autobiography of Parley P. Pratt*, p. 62.

31. *History of the Church*, 1:226.

32. Doctrine and Covenants 25:8

33. *History of the Church*, 1:85.

34. Doctrine and Covenants 87:1–4.

35. Milton V. Backman Jr., *The Heavens Resound: A History of the Latter-day Saints in Ohio, 1830–1838* (Salt Lake City: Deseret Book, 1983), p. 201; Painesville Telegraph, 7 February 1834, p. 3.

36. *History of the Church*, 3:231.

37. Doctrine and Covenants 42:33.

38. Marvin S. Hill, "The Shaping of the Mormon Mind in New England and New York," *Brigham Young University Studies*, vol. 9, no. 3 (Spring 1969), p. 368.

39. Stanley R. Gunn, *Oliver Cowdery, Second Elder and Scribe* (Salt Lake City: Bookcraft, 1962), p. 116; Huntington Library Letters, 10 May 1834.

40. Sidney Rigdon, *Elders' Journal*, vol. 1, no. 4 (August 1838), p. 54.

41. *Teachings of the Prophet Joseph Smith*, p. 79.

42. Ibid., pp. 79–80.

43. Leonard J. Arrington, "Joseph Smith, Builder of Ideal Communities," in Susan Easton Black and Larry Porter, eds., *The Prophet Joseph* (Salt Lake City: Deseret Book, 1988), p. 118.

44. "Newel Knight's Journal," *Scraps of Biography* (Salt Lake City: Juvenile Instructor Office, 1883), 10: 71.

45. Ibid., p. 72.

46. Arrington and Bitton, *The Mormon Experience*, p. 47.

47. Ibid., p. 44.

48. *History of the Church*, 1:457–58.

49. Ibid., pp. 453–56.

50. Hill, *Joseph Smith, the First Mormon*, p. 11.

51. Richard Bushman, "The Teachings of Joseph Smith," Annual Joseph Smith Memorial Sermons, LDS Institute of Religion, Logan, Utah, 18 January 1976.

5 A HOUSE OF GOD

1. Doctrine and Covenants 88:119.

2. *Discourses of Brigham Young*, sel. John A. Widtsoe (Salt Lake City: Deseret Book, 1954), p. 415.

3. *Journal of Discourses*, 17:273.

4. Doctrine and Covenants 38:32.

5. Pearson H. Corbett, *Hyrum Smith–Patriarch* (Salt Lake City: Deseret Book, 1963), p. 112.

6. Lucy Mack Smith, *History of Joseph Smith by His Mother*, ed. Preston Nibley (Salt Lake City: Bookcraft, 1954), p. 231.

7. See Statement of Joseph Millet, Sr., son of Artemus Millet, in "Ancestors and Descendants of Thomas Millett," LDS Church Archives.

8. Milton V. Backman Jr., *The Heavens Resound: A History of the Latter-day Saints in Ohio, 1830–1838* (Salt Lake City: Deseret Book, 1983), p. 28.

9. *Journal of Discourses*, 10:165.

10. Ibid., pp. 165–66.

11. Edward Tullidge, *The Women of Mormondom* (New York: Tullidge & Crandall, 1877), p. 76.

12. Donna Hill, *Joseph Smith, the First Mormon* (Garden City, NY: Doubleday and Co., 1977), p. 8.

13. Milton V. Backman Jr., "Truman Coe's Description of Mormonism," *Brigham Young University Studies*, vol. 17, no. 3 (Spring 1977), p. 355; quoting from Truman Coe, "Mormonism," *Cincinnati Journal and Western Luminary*, 25 August 1836, p. 4.

14. Ibid.

15. Orson F. Whitney, *Life of Heber C. Kimball, an Apostle; the Father and Founder of the British Mission* (Salt Lake City: Juvenile Instructor Office, 1888), p. 46.

16. Matthias F. Cowley, *Wilford Woodruff, History of His Life and Labors* (Salt Lake City: Bookcraft, 1964), p. 68.

17. *Journal of Discourses*, 2:31.

18. William W. Phelps, "The Spirit of God like a Fire Is Burning," *Hymns of The Church of Jesus Christ of Latter-day Saints* (Salt Lake City: The Church of Jesus Christ of Latter-day Saints, 1985), no. 2.

19. *History of the Church*, 2:428.

20. Orson Pratt, in *Journal of Discourses*, 18:132.

21. Tullidge, *Women of Mormondom*, p. 95.

22. As cited in Hyrum L. Andrus and Helen Mae Andrus, comp., *They Knew the Prophet* (Salt Lake City: Bookcraft, 1974), pp. 51–52.

23. Tullidge, *Women of Mormondom*, p. 207.

24. John Taylor, *The Gospel Kingdom*, sel. G. Homer Durham (Salt Lake City: Deseret Book, 1943), p. 122.

25. Doctrine and Covenants 110:2–3.

26. Doctrine and Covenants 110:7.

27. Mary Fielding Smith to her sister Mercy, 1 September 1837, in Kenneth W. Godfrey, Audrey M. Godfrey, and Jill Mulvay Derr, *Women's Voices* An Untold History of the Latter-day Saints, 1830–1900 (Salt Lake City: Deseret Book, 1982), p. 63.

28. Elden Jay Watson, *Manuscript History of Brigham Young 1801–1844* (Salt Lake City: Smith Secretarial Service, 1968), 1:16.

29. Interview with Ronald Esplin for *American Prophet: The Story of Joseph Smith*, 8 December 1998.

30. *Journal of Discourses*, 7:112.

31. *Journal of Discourses*, 7:114; Leonard J. Arrington and Davis Bitton, *The Mormon Experience* (Urbana and Chicago: University of Illinois Press, 1992), p. 67.

32. *Journal of Discourses*, 1:313.

33. *Journal of Discourses*, 11:295.

34. Leonard J. Arrington, ed., *Presidents of the Church* (Salt Lake City: Deseret Book, 1986), pp. 50–51.

35. *History of the Church*, 4:403.

36. *History of the Church*, 2:489.

37. Heber C. Kimball journal, as cited in Tullidge, *Women of Mormondom*, pp. 112–13.

38. Tullidge, *Women of Mormondom*, pp. 113–15.

39. J. Christopher Conkling, *A Joseph Smith Chronology* (Salt Lake City: Deseret Book, 1979), p. 101.

40. *History of the Church*, 2:488.

41. Milton V. Backman Jr., "Flight from Kirtland," in *Regional Studies in Latter-day Saint Church History—Ohio* (Provo, Utah: Dept. of Church History and Doctrine, Brigham Young University, 1990), p. 139.

42. Journal of John Smith, 23 April 1838, as cited in Liz Lemon Swindle and Susan Easton Black, *Joseph Smith: Impressions of a Prophet* (Salt Lake City: Deseret Book, 1998), p. 64.

6 A DARK, DIRTY PRISON

1. Leonard J. Arrington and Davis Bitton, *The Mormon Experience* (Urbana and Chicago: University of Illinois Press, 1992), p. 47.

2. Dean C. Jessee, ed., *The Papers of Joseph Smith: Autobiographical and Historical Writings*, 2 vols. (Salt Lake City: Deseret Book, 1989), 2:280.

3. Interview with Ronald Esplin for *American Prophet: The Story of Joseph Smith*, 8 December 1998.

4. Jessee, *Papers of Joseph Smith*, 2:280.

5. Ibid.

6. *History of the Church*, 3:167.

7. *History of the Church*, 6:241.

8. *History of the Church*, 1:468.

9. Oration Delivered by Mr. S. Rigdon, on the 4th of July, 1838 (Far West: Journal Office, 1838), 12; as cited in Peter Crawley, "Two Rare Missouri Documents," *Brigham Young University Studies*, vol. 14, no. 4 (Summer 1974), p. 527.

10. Parley P. Pratt, *Autobiography of Parley P. Pratt* (Salt Lake City: Deseret Book, 1985 ed.), p. 150.

11. *History of the Church*, 3:57.

12. Dean C. Jessee, ed., *The Personal Writings of Joseph Smith* (Salt Lake City: Deseret Book, 1984), p. 435.

13. Donna Hill, *Joseph Smith, the First Mormon* (Garden City, NY: Doubleday and Co., 1977), p. 230; *Jeffersonian Republican*, 22 September 1838.

14. *History of the Church*, 3:175.

15. Jessee, *Personal Writings of Joseph Smith*, p. 435.

16. *History of the Church*, 3:175.

17. *Biography or History of the Life and Times of Joseph Horne*, typescript in the author's possession, pp. 88–89.

18. *Journal of Discourses*, 23:37.

19. *Autobiography of Parley P. Pratt*, p. 159.

20. *Life and Times of Joseph Horne*, pp. 88–89.

21. *History of the Church*, 3:203.

22. *History of the Church*, 3:190–91.

23. *Journal of Discourses*, 17:92.

24. Ronald Esplin, "Joseph Smith's Mission and Timetable," in Susan Easton Black and Larry Porter, eds., *The Prophet Joseph* (Salt Lake City: Deseret Book, 1988), p. 298.

25. *Autobiography of Parley P. Pratt*, p. 180.

26. Ibid., pp. 159–60.

27. Ibid., p. 180.

28. Ivan J. Barrett, *Joseph Smith and the Restoration* (Provo, Utah: Brigham Young University Press, 1973), p. 420; John P. Greene, "Facts Relative to the Expulsion of the Mormons from the State of Missouri," microfilm, Harold B. Lee Library, Brigham Young University, Provo, Utah, p. 39.

29. *History of the Church*, 3:439.

30. *Journal of Discourses*, 3:269.

31. *Teachings of the Prophet Joseph Smith*, sel. Joseph Fielding Smith (Salt Lake City: Deseret Book, 1977), pp. 196–97.

32. As cited in Leonard J. Arrington, *Charles C. Rich* (Provo, Utah: Brigham Young University Press, 1974), p. 69.

33. Lucy Mack Smith, *History of Joseph Smith by His Mother*, ed. Preston Nibley (Salt Lake City: Bookcraft, 1954), pp. 190–91.

34. Jessee, *Personal Writings of Joseph Smith*, p. 425; spelling corrected.

35. Emma Smith to Joseph Smith, 7 March 1839, in Joseph Smith Letterbook, 2:37, LDS Church Archives.

36. Jessee, *Personal Writings of Joseph Smith*, p. 408; spelling corrected.

37. Jessee, *Personal Writings of Joseph Smith*, pp. 388–89; Emma Smith to Joseph Smith, 7 March 1839.

38. *Autobiography of Parley P. Pratt*, p. 188.

39. Mercy R. Thompson, "Recollections of the Prophet Joseph Smith," *Juvenile Instructor*, vol. 27, no. 13 (1 July 1892), p. 398.

40. "Liberty Jail, Missouri, Dec. 16, 1838," *Times and Seasons* 1:83–86.

41. Interview with Leonard J. Arrington for *American Prophet: The Story of Joseph Smith*, 20 October 1998.

42. Jessee, *Personal Writings of Joseph Smith*, p. 394.

43. Doctrine and Covenants 121:1–3.

44. Doctrine and Covenants 121:7–9.

45. "Hyrum Smith to the Saints scattered abroad," *Times and Seasons* 1:23. This is also the source for the quote across the middle of the page.

46. Jessee, *Personal Writings of Joseph Smith*, p. 110.

47. Ibid., p. 441.

48. *History of the Church*, 3:423.

49. Andrew F. Ehat and Lyndon W. Cook, comps., *The Words of Joseph Smith: The Contemporary Account of the Nauvoo Discourses of the Prophet Joseph* (Orem, Utah: Grandin Book Co., 1993), p. 192.

7 NAUVOO THE BEAUTIFUL

1. *History of the Church*, 3:375.

2. Ora H. Barlow, *The Israel Barlow Story* (Salt Lake City: Ora H. Barlow, 1968), p. 163.

3. Hyrum L. Andrus and Helen Mae Andrus, comp., *They Knew the Prophet* (Salt Lake City: Bookcraft, 1974), p. 41.

4. *History of the Church*, 4:3–4, fn.

5. Andrew F. Ehat and Lyndon W. Cook, comps., *The Words of Joseph Smith: The Contemporary Account of the Nauvoo Discourses of the Prophet Joseph* (Orem, Utah: Grandin Book Co., 1993), p. 124.

6. Edwin F. Parry, *Stories about Joseph Smith the Prophet* (Salt Lake City: Deseret News Press, 1934), pp. 33–34.

7. Matthias F. Cowley, *Wilford Woodruff, History of His Life and Labors* (Salt Lake City: Bookcraft, 1964), p. 104.

8. Ibid., p. 105.

9. *History of the Church*, 4:191–92.

10. *History of the Church*, 4:190.

11. George Peck, *The Life and Times of Rev. George Peck, D.D., written by himself* (New York: Nelson and Phillips, 1874), pp. 201–2.

12. See Stanley B. Kimball, "Nauvoo," *Improvement Era* 65 (July 1962): 548.

13. James Leech, *Juvenile Instructor*, vol. 27, no. 5 (1 March 1892), p. 152.

14. *History of the Church*, 6:367.

15. Interview with Leonard J. Arrington for *American Prophet: The Story of Joseph Smith*, 20 October 1998.

16. Donna Hill, *Joseph Smith, the First Mormon* (Garden City, NY: Doubleday and Co., 1977),

p. 292; James Gordon Bennett, in *New York Herald*, 14 November 1841.

17. *History of the Church*, 4:273.

18. Andrus and Andrus, *They Knew the Prophet*, p. 153.

19. Mary Ann Winters, "Joseph Smith, The Prophet," *Young Woman's Journal*, vol. 16, no. 12 (December 1905), p. 558.

20. Mary Frost Adams, *Young Woman's Journal*, vol. 16, no. 12 (December 1905), p. 538.

21. Marvin S. Hill, "Joseph Smith the Man: Some Reflections on a Subject of Controversy," *Brigham Young University Studies*, vol. 21, no. 2 (Spring 1981), p. 179.

22. Mercy R. Thompson, *Juvenile Instructor*, vol. 27, no. 13 (1 July 1892), p. 399.

23. Dean C. Jessee, ed., *The Personal Writings of Joseph Smith* (Salt Lake City: Deseret Book, 1984), p. 263.

24. *Teachings of the Prophet Joseph Smith*, sel. Joseph Fielding Smith (Salt Lake City: Deseret Book, 1977), p. 231.

25. *Discourses of Brigham Young*, sel. John A. Widtsoe (Salt Lake City: Deseret Book, 1954), p. 458.

26. *History of the Church*, 4:10, fn.

27. *History of the Church*, 4:10.

28. Leah D. Widtsoe, *Brigham Young, The Man of the Hour* (Salt Lake City: Bookcraft, 1947), pp. 87–88.

29. Robert Bruce Flanders, *Nauvoo: Kingdom on the Mississippi* (Urbana and Chicago: University of Illinois Press, 1965), p. 71.

30. Emmeline Blanche Wells, "Joseph Smith, The Prophet," *Young Woman's Journal*, vol. 16, no. 12 (December 1905), 555.

31. *History of the Church*, 6:300.

32. Flanders, *Kingdom on the Mississippi*, p. 2.

33. Flanders, *Kingdom on the Mississippi*, p. 147.

34. Jane James, "Joseph Smith, The Prophet," *Young Woman's Journal*, vol. 16, no. 12 (December 1905), p. 552.

35. Parry, *Stories about Joseph Smith*, pp. 127–28.

36. Jane Snyder Richards, "Joseph Smith, The Prophet," *Young Woman's Journal*, vol. 16, no. 12 (December 1905), p. 550.

37. Parry, *Stories about Joseph Smith*, pp. 23–24.

38. Winters, "Joseph Smith, The Prophet," p. 557.

39. Harvey Cluff Autobiography, typescript, p. 6, Brigham Young University.

40. Ehat and Cook, *Words of Joseph Smith*, p. 34.

41. *Teachings of the Prophet Joseph Smith*, p. 93.

42. Pearson H. Corbett, *Hyrum Smith–Patriarch* (Salt Lake City: Deseret Book, 1963), p. 268.

43. Enoch E. Dodge, *Young Woman's Journal*, vol. 16, no. 12 (December 1905), p. 544.

44. Calvin W. Moore, *Juvenile Instructor*, vol. 27, no. 8 (15 April 1892), p. 255.

45. Jill Mulvay Derr, Janath Russell Cannon, and Maureen Ursenbach Beecher, *Women of Covenant: The Story of Relief Society* (Salt Lake City: Deseret Book, 1992), p. 30.

46. Relief Society Minutes of Nauvoo, 17 March 1842, typescript, LDS Church Archives.

47. Derr, Cannon, and Beecher, *Women of Covenant*, p. 34.

48. Jessee, *Personal Writings of Joseph Smith*, p. 485.

49. Ibid.

50. As cited in Leonard J. Arrington and Davis Bitton, *The Mormon Experience* (Urbana and Chicago: University of Illinois Press, 1992), p. 71.

8 UNTIL MY TIME COMES

1. *Teachings of the Prophet Joseph Smith*, sel. Joseph Fielding Smith (Salt Lake City: Deseret Book, 1977), p. 274.

2. Dean C. Jessee, ed., *The Personal Writings of Joseph Smith* (Salt Lake City: Deseret Book, 1984), p. 484.

3. *History of the Church*, 6:197.

4. *History of the Church*, 7:434.

5. Doctrine and Covenants 132:46.

6. *History of the Church*, 5:1–2.

7. Parley P. Pratt, *Autobiography of Parley P. Pratt* (Salt Lake City: Deseret Book, 1985 ed.), p. 60.

8. As cited in Barbara Fluckiger Watt, "Bathsheba Bigler Smith: Woman of Faith and Courage," in Vicky Burgess-Olson, ed., *Sister Saints* (Provo, Utah: Brigham Young University Press, 1978), p. 206.

9. *Journal of Discourses*, 3:266.

10. As cited in Ronald Esplin, "Joseph Smith's Mission and Timetable," in Susan Easton Black and Larry Porter, eds., *The Prophet Joseph* (Salt Lake City: Deseret Book, 1988), p. 303; spelling corrected.

11. Interview with Jan Shipps for *American Prophet: The Story of Joseph Smith*, 17 December 1998.

12. Interview with Ronald Esplin for *American Prophet: The Story of Joseph Smith*, 8 December 1998.

13. *History of the Church*, 5:401.

14. Daniel Tyler, *Juvenile Instructor*, vol. 27, no. 16 (15 August 1892), p. 492.

15. *Teachings of the Prophet Joseph Smith*, p. 313.

16. Alvah Alexander, "Joseph Smith, The Prophet," *Young Woman's Journal*, vol. 17, no. 12 (December 1906), p. 541.

17. *History of the Church*, 4:587–88.

18. *Autobiography of Parley P. Pratt*, p. 32.

19. Richard Neitzel Holzapfel and Jeni Broberg Holzapfel, *Women of Nauvoo* (Salt Lake City: Bookcraft, 1992), p. 103; Sarah Hall Scott to Abigail Hall, 16 June 1844.

20. *History of the Church*, 6:185.

21. Interview with Dallin Oaks for *American Prophet: The Story of Joseph Smith*, 7 December 1998.

22. George Q. Cannon, *Life of Joseph Smith the Prophet* (Salt Lake City: Deseret Book, 1986), p. 345; James Gordon Bennett, *New York Herald*, 3 April 1842.

23. *History of the Church*, 6:346.

24. *Teachings of the Prophet Joseph Smith*, p. 345.

25. See Donald Q. Cannon, "The King Follett Discourse: Joseph Smith's Greatest Sermon in Historical Perspective," *Brigham Young University Studies*, vol. 18, no. 2 (Winter 1978), p. 179.

26. Ibid., p. 190; *Warsaw Signal*, 10 April 1844.

27. Robert Bruce Flanders, *Nauvoo: Kingdom on the Mississippi* (Urbana and Chicago: University of Illinois Press, 1965), p. 267. Those who signed the statement included Joseph D. Conoly, Mary Ann Conoly, Mary A. Converce, Robert Angould, Martha Angould, Charles Chase, Jr., Richard Chase, Sarah McMullen, E. H. McMullen, H.H.Ogle, Sr.

28. See Cannon, "The King Follett Discourse," p. 189; *Nauvoo Expositor*, 7 June 1844.

29. *History of the Church*, 6:3.

30. Jessee, *The Personal Writings of Joseph Smith*, p. 548; spelling corrected.

31. Ibid.; spelling corrected.

32. *History of the Church*, 4:480.

33. Leonard J. Arrington and Davis Bitton, *The Mormon Experience* (Urbana and Chicago: University of Illinois Press, 1992), p. 52; William Harris, *Mormonism Portrayed; Its Errors and Absurdities* (Warsaw, Illinois: n. p., 1841), p. 15.

34. Cannon, *Life of Joseph Smith*, p. 370.

35. *History of the Church*, 6:5.

36. *Warsaw Signal*, 29 May 1844.

37. *Warsaw Signal*, 12 June 1844, p. 2; *History of the Church*, 6:xxxix.

38. *History of the Church*, 6:540.

39. *Teachings of the Prophet Joseph Smith*, p. 376.

40. Hyrum L. Andrus and Helen Mae Andrus, comp., *They Knew the Prophet* (Salt Lake City: Bookcraft, 1974), p. 184.

41. *History of the Church*, 558, 555.

42. *History of the Church*, 6:605.

EPILOGUE

1. *Teachings of the Prophet Joseph Smith*, sel. Joseph Fielding Smith (Salt Lake City: Deseret Book, 1977), p. 361.

2. Dean C. Jessee, ed., *The Personal Writings of Joseph Smith* (Salt Lake City: Deseret Book, 1984), p. 544.

3. Ibid., pp. 218–19.

4. Statement by B.H. Roberts, as cited in Truman Madsen, *Joseph Smith the Prophet* (Salt Lake City: Bookcraft, 1989), p.116.

5. Doctrine and Covenants 135:3.

6. *Journal of Discourses*, 9:332.

7. *Journal of Discourses*, 3:51.

8. Josiah Quincy, *Figures of the Past* (Boston: Roberts Brothers, 1884), p. 376.

PHOTOGRAPHS
AND ILLUSTRATIONS

The following images have all been used by permission. We gratefully acknowledge the help of Bill Slaughter and April Williamsen for the images from the Historical Department, Archives Division, of The Church of Jesus Christ of Latter-day Saints, cited below as LDS Church Historical Department. Glen Leonard and Ron Read from the Museum of Church History and Art provided many of the Joseph Smith portraits and allowed access for us to photograph other artifacts. Many thanks also to Dr. Cynthia Lee Henthorn, Visual Culture Historian at the City College of New York, who gathered archival images from a multitude of sources.

Page 4, Gregory Peck, photograph © Susan Gray. Joseph Smith, drawing by Danquart A. Weggeland, *Contributor* magazine, 1886. Image courtesy Museum of Church History and Art.

Page 5, Joseph Smith portraits: bottom left, engraving by Frederick Piercy, image courtesy Museum of Church History and Art; center, painting by Del Parson, © 1998; top right, painting by Lewis Ramsey, image courtesy Museum of Church History and Art.

Page 6, Joseph Smith portraits: left, pencil sketch attributed to Frederick Piercy, image courtesy

Museum of Church History and Art; right, painting by unknown artist, image courtesy Reorganized Church of Jesus Christ of Latter Day Saints Library Archives.

Pages 8–9, Wagon with coffins, photograph © John Snyder.

Page 10, Joseph Smith, painting by unknown artist. Image courtesy Reorganized Church of Jesus Christ of Latter Day Saints Library Archives.

Page 11, Carthage Jail, photograph © Lauri Eskelson. Inset of pistol, photograph © John Snyder, courtesy Museum of Church History and Art.

Page 12, John Taylor's watch, photograph courtesy Museum of Church History and Art. Carthage Jail interior, photograph © John Snyder.

Pages 12–13, Woman at window, photograph © John Snyder.

Page 13, Willard Richards, photograph courtesy LDS Church Historical Department. Wagon driver, photograph © John Snyder.

Page 14, Mansion House, photograph courtesy LDS Church Historical Department.

Page 15, Martyrdom sampler, created by Mary Ann Broomhead. Image courtesy Museum of Church History and Art.

Pages 16–17, Mourners, photograph © John Snyder.

Page 18, Carthage Jail, photograph courtesy LDS Church Historical Department.

Page 19, Martyrdom at Carthage, engraving, from Vergilius Ferm, *Pictorial History of Protestantism: A Panoramic View of Western Europe and the United States* (New York: Philosophical Library, 1957). Image courtesy LDS Church Historical Department.

Page 20, Joseph Smith, engraving by Frederick Piercy. Image courtesy Museum of Church History and Art.

Page 21, Dallin H. Oaks, photograph © Lauri Eskelson. Governor Thomas Ford, image courtesy LDS Church Historical Department.

Pages 22–23, Smith home, photograph © Lauri Eskelson.

Page 24, Joseph Smith, pencil sketch attributed to Frederick Piercy. Image courtesy Museum of Church History and Art.

Page 25, Benjamin Franklin, Thomas Jefferson, George

Washington, images courtesy New York Public Library Picture Collection, Mid-Manhattan Branch.

Page 26, "Up Out of the Baptismal Waters," engraving by unknown artist. Image courtesy American Baptist Historical Society, Rochester, New York. Frontier church, photograph by Walker Evans. Image courtesy Library of Congress and Metropolitan Museum of Art Walker Evans Collection.

Page 27, Vermont pioneers, image courtesy New York Public Library Picture Collection, Mid-Manhattan Branch.

Page 29, St. John's Evangelical Lutheran Church, Rochester, NY, image courtesy Rochester Public Library, Local History Section, and Museum Photographics, Rochester, NY.

Page 30, David Whittaker, photograph © Lee Groberg.

Page 31, "View on the Erie Canal," painting by John William Hill, image courtesy Stokes Collection, Prints Div., New York Public Library, Fifth Avenue and 42nd Street, New York, NY 10018–2788.

Page 32, Gordon Wood, photograph © Lee Groberg.

Page 33, Grove of trees, photograph © John Snyder.

Pages 34–35, Sacred Grove, photograph © John Snyder.

Page 36, Joseph Smith, drawing by Danquart A. Weggeland, *Contributor* magazine, 1886. Image courtesy Museum of Church History and Art.

Page 37, "Religious Camp Meeting," painting by J. Maze Burbank, image courtesy Old Dartmouth Historical Society/New Bedford Whaling Museum. Nathan Hatch, photograph © Lee Groberg.

Pages 38–39, Four steeples, photograph © John Snyder.

Page 41, Sacred Grove, photograph by George Edward Anderson. Image courtesy LDS Church Historical Department.

Page 42, Gordon B Hinckley, photograph © Drake Busath.

Page 43, Joseph Smith's First Vision, stained glass, maker unknown, on display at Museum of Church History and Art, Salt Lake City, Utah. Image courtesy Museum of Church History and Art.

Page 45, Trees, photograph © John Snyder.

Page 47, M. Russell Ballard, photograph © Lee Groberg.

Page 48, Emma Hale Smith, painting by unknown artist. Image courtesy Reorganized Church of Jesus Christ of Latter Day Saints Library Archives.

Page 49, Hill Cumorah and Smith family home, photographs by George Edward Anderson. Images courtesy LDS Church Historical Department.

Pages 50–51, Writing table with quill pen, photograph © John Snyder.

Page 52, Joseph Smith, painting by Lewis Ramsey. Image courtesy Museum of Church History and Art.

Page 53, Trees on Hill Cumorah, photograph © John Snyder.

Pages 54–55, Joseph Smith's home in Harmony, Pennsylvania, photograph by George Edward Anderson. Image courtesy LDS Church Historical Department.

Page 56, Columbia College, New York, 1830 engraving, image courtesy Columbia University Archives and Columbiana Library. Emma Smith's ring, photograph © John Snyder, courtesy Reorganized Church of Jesus Christ of Latter Day Saints.

Page 59, The Three Witnesses to the Book of Mormon, engraving by Charles B. Hall. Image courtesy LDS Church Historical Department.

Page 60, David Whitmer portrait, image courtesy Reorganized Church of Jesus Christ of Latter Day Saints. Robert Millet, photograph © Lee Groberg.

Page 61, Richard Hughes, photograph © Lee Groberg. Grandin Book building, photograph © John Snyder.

Page 62, Antique copies of Book of Mormon, photograph © John Snyder, courtesy Museum of Church History and Art.

Page 63, Hot lead type in Grandin Book building, photograph © John Snyder.

Page 64, W. W. Phelps, image courtesy LDS Church Historical Department.

Page 65, Mario DePillis, photograph © Lee Groberg. Book of Mormon, image courtesy Museum of Church History and Art.

Pages 66–67, Wagon train, photograph © Lauri Eskelson.

Page 68, Joseph Smith, painting attributed to Danquart A. Weggeland. Image courtesy Museum of Church History and Art.

Page 69, Susquehanna River, photograph by George Edward Anderson. Image courtesy LDS Church Historical Department.

Pages 70–71, Susquehanna River, photograph © John Snyder.

Page 72, Orson Hyde, image courtesy LDS Church Historical Department.

Page 74, Map of Kirtland, Ohio, area, courtesy Paul Jager. © 1999 Seeing Eye Studios, Inc.

Page 75, Wagon train, photograph © Lauri Eskelson.

Page 76, John Johnson, image courtesy LDS Church Historical Department. Richard Bushman, photograph © Lee Groberg.

Page 77, Sidney Rigdon, Parley P. Pratt, images courtesy LDS Church Historical Department.

Page 79, Newel K. Whitney's store, image courtesy LDS Church Historical Department. Hyrum Smith's Hebrew Bible, first LDS hymnal, and transcript of revelation (background), photographs © John Snyder, courtesy Museum of Church History and Art.

Jan Shipps, photograph © Lee Groberg.

Page 81, "A Franklin County, Ohio, Farm Scene," image courtesy Ohio Historical Society, Archives/Library Division, 1982 Velma Avenue, Columbus, OH 43211–2497.

Pages 82–83, "Mormons Building a Bridge," engraving, *Harper's Magazine* 6 (April 1853): 616. Image courtesy Reorganized Church of Jesus Christ of Latter Day Saints Library Archives.

Page 84, "Mormon Troubles in Missouri Begin," engraving in T.B.H. Stenhouse, *The Rocky Mountain Saints* (New York: D. Appleton and Co., 1873), p. 81. Image courtesy Reorganized Church of Jesus Christ of Latter Day Saints Library Archives.

Page 85, "Mt. Sterling, Missouri, Ferry," image courtesy Jefferson National Expansion Memorial, Museum of Westward Expansion, 11 North Fourth Street, St. Louis, MO 63102.

Pages 86–87, Kirtland Temple windows, photograph © John Snyder, courtesy Reorganized Church of Jesus Christ of Latter Day Saints.

Page 88, Joseph Smith, photograph of painting, retouched by Danquart A. Weggeland. Image courtesy Museum of Church History and Art.

Page 89, Kirtland Temple, exterior and interior shots, photographs © John Snyder, courtesy Reorganized Church of Jesus Christ of Latter Day Saints.

Page 90, Kirtland Temple window, photograph © John Snyder, courtesy Reorganized Church of Jesus Christ of Latter Day Saints.

Page 91, Scissors, thimble, and thread, photograph © John Snyder, courtesy Museum of Church History and Art.

Page 92, "The Spirit of God," in LDS hymnal, image courtesy Museum of Church History and Art.

Page 93, Pulpits in Kirtland Temple, photograph © John Snyder, courtesy Reorganized Church of Jesus Christ of Latter Day Saints.

Page 94, Eliza R. Snow, image courtesy LDS Church Historical Department.

Page 95, Kirtland landscape, photograph by George Edward Anderson. Image courtesy LDS Church Historical Department.

Page 96, Martin Marty, photograph © Lee Groberg.

Page 97, Heber C. Kimball, image courtesy LDS Church Historical Department.

Page 98, Brigham Young, image courtesy LDS Church Historical Department.

Page 99, Kirtland Safety Society note, photograph courtesy Reorganized Church of Jesus Christ of Latter Day Saints.

Pages 100–101, Prisoner in chains, photograph © Lauri Eskelson.

Page 102, Joseph Smith, painting by Henri Moser. Image courtesy Museum of Church History and Art.

Page 103, Rural farming scene, image courtesy State Historical Society of Missouri, 1020 Lowry Street, Columbia, MO 65201-7298.

Pages 104-5, Missouri sunset, photograph © John Snyder.

Page 106, Antique rifles, images courtesy Museum of Church History and Art. "Massacre of Mormons at Haun's Mill," image courtesy State Historical Society of Missouri, 1020 Lowry Street, Columbia, MO 65201-7298.

Page 107, Alexander Doniphan, image courtesy LDS Church Historical Department.

Page 108, Jail door, photograph © John Snyder, courtesy Reorganized Church of Jesus Christ of Latter Day Saints.

Pages 108-9, Liberty Jail, image courtesy LDS Church Historical Department.

Page 109, Brigham Young, image courtesy LDS Church Historical Department.

Page 110, Crossing the frozen Mississippi, photograph © John Snyder. Gravestone, photograph by George Edward Anderson. Image courtesy LDS Church Historical Department.

Page 111, Emma Smith photo and mementos, photograph © John Snyder, courtesy Reorganized Church of Jesus Christ of Latter Day Saints.

Page 113, Joseph Smith letter, image courtesy LDS Church Historical Department. Inkwell and quill pen, photograph © John Snyder, courtesy Museum of Church History and Art.

Page 114, Tree in moonlight, photograph © John Snyder.

Page 117, Hyrum Smith, painting by Lewis Ramsey. Image courtesy Museum of Church History and Art.

Pages 118-19, Nauvoo, Illinois, lithograph, image courtesy LDS Church Historical Department.

Page 120, Joseph Smith, painting by Peter Kamps. Image courtesy Museum of Church History and Art. John Smith, image courtesy LDS Church Historical Department.

Page 121, Marsh with geese, photograph © John Snyder.

Page 123, Nauvoo from across the Mississippi River, photograph by George Edward Anderson. Image courtesy LDS Church Historical Department. Nauvoo city plat, image courtesy LDS Church Historical Department. Wheelbarrow, photograph © Lauri Eskelson.

Page 124, Robert Remini, photograph © Lee Groberg.

Page 125, Nauvoo Legion Benevolent Association banner, painting by Danquart A. Weggeland. Image courtesy Museum of Church History and Art.

Page 126, Joseph preaching, photograph © Lauri Eskelson.

Page 127, Missionaries, photograph © Lauri Eskelson.

Page 128, Joseph Smith, photograph of painting, retouched by Danquart A. Weggeland. Image courtesy Museum of Church History and Art.

Page 129, Baptism at River Ribble, photograph © Jonathan Groberg.

Page 130, Leonard J. Arrington, photograph © Stephen Moody. Image courtesy Heidi Swinton.

Pages 130-31, Child's top and marbles, photograph © John Snyder, courtesy Museum of Church History and Art.

Page 131, Main Street in Nauvoo, image courtesy LDS Church Historical Department.

Page 132, Joseph Smith, engraving by Frederick Piercy. Image courtesy Museum of Church History and Art.

Page 133, Nauvoo Seventies Hall, photograph © John Snyder.

Page 134, Elaine Jack, photograph © Lee Groberg.

Page 135, Key, photograph © John Snyder, courtesy Museum of Church History and Art.

Pages 136-37, Storm clouds, stock image courtesy of Photodisc.

Page 138, Joseph Smith, engraving by Frederick Piercy. Image courtesy Museum of Church History and Art.

Page 139, Nauvoo Temple, image courtesy LDS Church Historical Department.

Page 140, Bathsheba Smith, painting by Lee Greene Richards. Image courtesy Heidi Swinton.

Page 142, Larry Moore, photograph © Lee Groberg.

Page 143, Ross Peterson, photograph © Lee Groberg.

Page 145, View of Mississippi River through trees, photograph © John Snyder.

Page 146, Handbill promoting Joseph Smith for president, inset of Book of Commandments, photographs © John Snyder, courtesy Museum of Church History and Art.

Page 148, Lieutenant General Joseph Smith, painting by Sutcliffe Maudsley. Image courtesy Museum of Church History and Art.

Page 149, General Joseph Smith and Nauvoo Legion, painting by John Hafen (image flopped). Image courtesy Museum of Church History and Art. Insets of office nameplate, eagle-head sword handle, photographs © John Snyder, courtesy Museum of Church History and Art.

Page 150, Joseph Smith's watch, photograph © John Snyder, courtesy Reorganized Church of Jesus Christ of Latter Day Saints.

Page 151, Procession to Carthage, photograph © Jonathan Groberg.

Page 152, Joseph Smith, painting by Del Parson, © 1998.

Art Direction and Design: Scott Eggers
Principal Photography: John Snyder
Archival Imaging: Michael Schoenfeld
Digital Design: Dennis Millard